**Barry
Shafer**

SEE, BELIEVE, LIVE

An Inductive Study in John

ZONDERVAN®

ZONDERVAN.com/
AUTHORTRACKER
follow your favorite authors

**youth
specialties**

**youth
specialties**

See, Believe, Live: An Inductive Study in John
Copyright 2008 by InWord Resources, Inc.

Youth Specialties resources, 300 S. Pierce St., El Cajon, CA 92020 are published by Zondervan, 5300 Patterson Ave. SE, Grand Rapids, MI 49530.

Published in association with literary agency of WordServe Literary Group, Ltd., 10152 S. Knoll Ciricle, Highlands Ranch, CO 80130.

Library of Congress Cataloging-in-Publication Data

Shafer, Barry, 1961-
  See, believe, live : an inductive study in John / Barry Shafer.
    p. cm. — (Digging deeper series)
  ISBN 978-0-310-27498-8 (pbk.)
 1. Bible. N.T. John—Textbooks. 2. Bible. N.T. John—Study and teaching.
3. Youth—Religious life—Textbooks. 4. Youth—Religious life—Study and teaching. I. Title.
  BS2616.S53 2008
  226.5'077—dc22

2008026388

Cover design by Toolbox Studios
Interior design by SharpSeven Design

Printed in the United States of America

08 09 10 11 12 13 14 15 16 17 • 20 19 18 17 16 15 14 13 12 11 10 9 8 7 6 5 4 3 2 1

ACKNOWLEDGMENTS

As you'd expect, a Bible study of this scope could not have happened without the backing of an awesome team. Thank you to the many people who helped bring this project to fruition. They include Mary Huebner, for lending her middle school know-how, and Sean Michael Murphy, for letting us borrow his "talk" expertise. The Youth Specialties/Zondervan team: Heather Campbell, whose tireless efforts and attention to detail made this a better Bible study; Roni Meek, for graciously keeping the team on track; and Jay Howver, for taking seriously the need and desire for depth in youth ministry.

A big thanks to my scholar-friend Tom Thatcher, who has helped me appreciate the message of the Gospel through the eyes of the apostle John. Thank you to Jim Hancock for his encouragement and for inspiring a Bible study of this scope.

A big thanks to my wife, Dana, who makes me a better writer, studier, and follower of Christ.

And to you, the youth worker, who has picked up a Bible study with the word "deeper" in its series title. Thank you for your heart for students and for connecting them to God's Word.

Barry Shafer

TABLE OF CONTENTS

Session 9: Sole Mates (John 13)

Session 10: Famous Last Words (John 14)

Session 11: Pilate's Plot (John 18–19)

Session 12: Resurrection (John 20)

INTRODUCTION

For John it was black and white. Light and dark. Why? Because the people of his day were making organized, intentional efforts to accentuate the gray areas about Jesus, to explain him in more human, less incarnational terms. Sound familiar? The Christmas and Easter issues of every major news magazine these days carry themes along the lines of, "Rethinking Jesus," or "In Search of the Historical Jesus," with *historical* meaning "human, not divine." The message of this book may be more urgent now than ever.

John uses his favorite word, *believe*, more than 75 times in his Gospel, more than the other three Gospel writers combined. The people of Jesus' time didn't casually throw this word around. They understood that belief changes people's actions. A person's belief would be evident by his behavior. With his prolific use of this word, John is definitely making a point here, and this study ensures students won't miss it.

As you move through the Gospel of John teachable moment by teachable moment, you and your students will come face-to-face with Jesus, not only in the pages of the Bible, but also in the events of your week.

Through this study, students will—

- jettison any underused, out-of-date pictures of Jesus they have lying around in their hearts.
- discover that no one has a greater interest in their spiritual well-being than Jesus.
- be inspired, encouraged, and certainly intrigued by the colorful characters they'll see interacting with Jesus, such as Nicodemus, Mary, Martha, a man blind from birth, Jewish leaders, curious onlookers, committed followers, and not-so-committed followers.
- rearrange their worlds to accept the big challenges in John's Gospel: Love one another, be unified, and believe in Jesus as the Christ.

Digging Deeper Series

Today's postmodern students are seeking depth. They are probing Christianity and other faiths, checking to see which faith demands and delivers spiritual depth. The deepest often wins. The

Digging Deeper series, a result of collaborative efforts between Youth Specialties and InWord Resources, will give adult leaders everything they need to satisfy their students' craving for depth, while leaving them wanting more of God's word in their lives. Deeper Bible study has never been more accessible. Or more rewarding.

Every session contains a personal study (Prep It) to guide you, the leader, through the Scripture in a way that still leaves plenty of room for self-discovery. You then choose one of six different session guides (Teach It) from the accompanying CD-ROM. Each guide is targeted for a different age and setting. Leading middle school? Got it! High schoolers at Starbucks? Covered. College age? Got that, too. Need a talk? Here you go. The Teach It guide serves as your cue sheet for navigating the group session.

The Prep It feature helps leaders, whether nervous rookies or seasoned vets, gain competence and confidence in taking on what can appear to be a daunting task: leading students in deeper Bible study. The multiple session options ensure an approach designed specifically for your students.

But there's more. Each study in the Digging Deeper series comes with its own Web support, where you'll find even *more* session options, large-group ideas, user ideas, and constantly updated tie-ins with today's issues and events. You'll also find updated media suggestions (music, video clips) along with specific application and long-term follow-up ideas. Look for the Digging Deeper series icon. We've noted password info for *See, Believe, Live* in these instructions and throughout the Prep It study guides in this book.

It's a challenge for students to find quality personal time with God in their busy weeks, no matter how much you encourage that activity. The group sessions in the Digging Deeper series come with built-in solitude to help your students explore the great depths of Scripture. This guarantees that for at least a few minutes in their week, students are giving God a chance to speak into their lives. With your students fresh off personal discovery, group interaction promises to be invigorating as your students apply in community what they explored in solitude.

You'll soon find that this series offers more than an energizing hour of depth and discussion to help students through their week. Built on an inductive Bible study approach, the Digging Deeper series melds the postmodern student's diligent search for spiritual depth with God's promise of reward. As students experience God's Word and subtly learn time-tested Bible study tools, they'll lay a solid foundation for confident Bible study and accurate application of Scripture. In short, they'll discover how to listen and respond to God for the rest of their lives.

INSTRUCTIONS

What You Have Here

Each session contains a guided personal study for the group leader (Prep It) and six different types of session guides (Teach It) for you to choose from, based on the age and setting of your Bible study (middle school, younger high school, older high school, college age, coffeehouse or a talk). Once you've completed the Prep It, use the session outlines included in this book to choose the appropriate Teach It guide. We've noted descriptions of the guides below. The full Teach It guide for each session, with reproducible student journal pages and Scripture sheets, is on the accompanying CD-ROM.

Prep It

This is a guided personal study for the group leader. Because the most powerful teaching of God's Word flows out of the leader's personal experience in Scripture, this personal prep helps you *own* the scripture before meeting with your group. The Prep It for each session is included in this book; you'll find plenty of space to write your thoughts and discoveries. Allow about an hour for personal study some time before the session with your students.

Teach It

Found on the accompanying CD-ROM, the Teach It guide is the leader's cue sheet for leading the session. Teach It includes prompts and notes for moving the group through the exercises, as well as guidance for leading the group discussion. And you have options! Each session has six different Teach It guides from which the leader can choose based on students' ages and the setting of your group time. You'll find the student pages for each session with their respective Teach It guides.

The following design elements will help you navigate through Teach It:

> Some text is in normal type such as you're reading now. This font style indicates instructions and cues to help you move from one exercise to the next during the session.

Type like this indicates questions, stories, prompts, or points of discussion to raise with your group. You may read these questions word-for-word, or you may be more comfortable reframing the questions and points in your own words so you can be more responsive to answers and other comments your students make.

Type like this indicates suggested or sample responses, as well as possible observations from Scripture. In essence, this is the answer font.

This icon found on the student journal pages indicates exercises for students to do in solitude. The Teach It guide contains instructions for the leader to convey to the students before they begin their time alone. The instructions on the students' journal pages will then lead them in a guided personal retreat.

Teach It Descriptions

These descriptions will help you know which Teach It guide is best suited for your group.

- **Middle School:** This session is intended for grades six through eight and is appropriate for a small-group setting or Sunday school.

- **High School 1:** Of the two high school guides, High School 1 is more casual in its approach and is appropriate for high school Sunday school or students who aren't sure how committed they want to be to Bible study and discipleship. It's intended for grades nine through 12, but with a nod toward nine and 10. This guide is also appropriate for the larger teaching settings.

    LARGE-GROUP OPTION:
    In the High School 1 Teach It guides, look for sidebars with the label **LARGE-GROUP OPTION** for ideas on how to lead the session in a large group.

- **High School 2:** This session is intended for the high school student who is looking for depth and has perhaps "signed up" for a deeper experience. It's intended for grades nine through 12, but with a nod toward 11 and 12.

- **College Age:** This session is geared for young adults, whether in college or working a job. The content does assume some spiritual initiative or curiosity on the part of the students.

- **Coffeehouse:** Just what it says—a lighter approach for the coffeehouse or cafe setting, high school or college age. A couple of suggestions: napkins can make great journal pages, and your servers will appreciate a good tip.

- **Talk:** That's right, a talk guide! And it's just that: a guide. It's not intended to be a manuscript to read aloud. It's here to give you ideas, structure, and stories to blend with your personal study (Prep It) as you prepare a talk. The content complements the other Teach It guides, allowing you to give a talk on the same topic students are studying in other settings (such as small groups). For help with these talks, we brought in an expert, Young Life leader and former area director Sean Michael Murphy. Sean's personal stories are intended to spark your thinking for personal stories of your own. But if nothing "sparks," feel free to simply use one of Sean's stories and intro it by saying, "I read about someone who..."

How This Works

After you've completed the Prep It and chosen the appropriate Teach It guide, print the Teach It guide from the CD-ROM for use in the session. Also print or photocopy enough student pages for your group. Be sure to read through the Teach It guide so you're familiar with the flow of the session and confident with the exercises. This will also help you plan for any exercises that ask for advance preparation.

The Session

An integral part of this study is hands-on interaction with the text by marking key words, promises, instructions, and other phrases—which helps students observe important details that they might not uncover with a casual reading. Having bigger text and more space on the included Scripture sheets facilitates this process.

Your students will be using colored pencils to mark the text, so have a good supply available. Most sessions suggest having a couple of colors for each student. While not mandatory, students may find it helpful to use the same color or symbol (or both) from one session to the next when marking the same word or concept.

For example, a student may want to mark all references to God with a blue cloud. Another student may pick a different color but use the same symbol. In most cases we've suggested symbols, but you may want to ask your students for their ideas.

What You'll Need

For every session, you'll need the same basic materials: Bibles, pens, colored pencils, a whiteboard and markers, and copies of Scripture sheets and journal pages. It would be helpful to provide your students with three-ring notebooks for their Scripture sheets and journal pages. Naturally this will add a step to your prep—three-hole punching your student pages for the notebooks. For the coffeehouse setting and the talks, the materials needed will be a bit different.

Some sessions have options that require a few other supplies. It's a good idea to keep a data projector or computer screen handy, since at times you may need to project info or have Web access for video clips.[1] While you can download and play some video clips with a media viewer on your computer (such as Windows Media Player), you'll need to stream other clips from video-sharing Web sites such as YouTube. You'll see suggestions for video clips in the Teach It guides. (Given the temporary nature of Web links, we sometimes list specific links to videos, but also offer useful keywords for Web searches.)

Although we suggest using a whiteboard throughout the book, you can substitute a flip chart, butcher paper taped to the wall, or whatever works conveniently for you.

Web Support

If multiple session guides for you to choose from isn't enough, there's more! You can find additional resources and tie-ins for each session at www.inword.org. Here you'll find up-to-date media suggestions, additional study background, and more session ideas to help you customize the Bible-study experience for your students. At www.inword.org, look for the Digging Deeper icon and enter the following access information for *See, Believe, Live* when prompted:

> **user name:** Believe
> **password:** Johnny

Prayer Effort

The purpose of this study isn't to simply fill up the next few Wednesday nights in your student-ministry schedule. It's an opportunity for God to speak to your students through his Word. Therefore, the most important component of your preparation is prayer. We suggest that you organize a group of prayer partners—adults in your student ministry or church—who will pray specifically for your group's experience in this study.

Give these prayer partners the names of your group members, the time frame of the study, and any information that will help them pray specifically for you and your students. In fact, take five minutes now to gather the names and phone numbers of people who have an active prayer life and a heart for the students in your ministry. Then take another 10 minutes to call them, asking them to pray. Commit to staying in touch with your prayer partners, keeping them apprised of your study content and your students' needs. This will also help you stay purposeful in personally praying for your students.

The impact of your Bible study is directly related to the prayer surrounding the study time with your students. We encourage you to make prayer a key part of your personal preparation and your student sessions. God's Spirit is what keeps God's Word from simply being dry words on a page. Open each session asking God's Spirit to soften your students' hearts. Close each session with a commitment to respond to what God has put on each student's heart.

---

1 Before you show video clips to your students, it might be a good idea to check out the Church Video License Web site www. cvli.com/about/index.cfm and Christian Copyright Licensing International www.ccli.com/usa/default.aspx to make sure you are complying with copyright laws.

SESSION 1

Setting the Heart

Remember the "eureka" moment—the day, the week, or the phase of life—when the message of the gospel first got through to you? For generations church leaders have given us loads of words for that moment: "born again," "accepted Christ," "saved," and so on. But no matter what label you use, the bottom line is that *you* had an encounter with Jesus Christ that totally transformed your life!

There was a time in history when the message of the gospel was brand-new—no clichés, no man-made traditions, no worn-out analogies—simply the pure actions and words of Jesus. As Jesus walked throughout the regions of Judea, Samaria, and Galilee, "eureka" moments were happening everywhere. Here's one example:

> Then Jesus went back across the Jordan to the place where John had been baptizing in the early days. Here he stayed and many people came to him. They said, "Though John never performed a miraculous sign, all that John said about this man was true." And in that place many believed in Jesus. (John 10:40-42)

This first session is designed to give you a big-picture look at the Gospel of John. This will provide an important framework, giving you a place to hook the teachable moments you'll experience throughout this study. Take a few moments to prepare your heart for an encounter with Jesus— an encounter that will bring you fresh "eureka" moments with the Savior.

Digging In

Purpose Statement

Many Bible authors come right out and tell their readers the reasons why they wrote what they did. Some of these "purpose statements" are obvious in Scripture, while others take some digging to discover. John's reason for writing his Gospel is one of the most explicitly stated in all of the Bible's 66 books—it shows up in nearly every chapter.

Enough talk. Let's dive in. Read the verses referenced below from your Bible. As you read, keep track of *who* did *what*, and note this info in the table. When you've finished observing these passages, take a minute to see if a theme—or purpose—of this book of the Bible emerges. Write your conclusions in the space provided.

	Who... did what?
John 2:22	
John 4:39	
John 9:35-38	
John 11:23-27	
John 20:30-31	

Your concluding thoughts on the theme of John:

Hope you got it (before you wrote a two-page paper on the theme of John!) that John spells out his theme in John 20:30-31. No guesswork needed! But let's take a closer look.

John 20:30-31 is printed on your Scripture sheet. Take a moment to examine this passage carefully by doing the following:

1. Circle the reason *why* "these" things are written.

2. Underline to *whom* "these" things are written.

3. Draw a box around *what* John wants us to believe.

4. Draw fireworks ✹ (be creative!) around what happens *when* we believe.

What appears to be the *key word* in this passage and the others you just read? (Incidentally, this key word unlocks the theme of the entire book.)

Insight

Believing Is Believing

The key word that gives insight into the reason John wrote his Gospel is *believe*. John uses this word more frequently than the other three Gospels writers combined.[2] We're thinking God wanted to get a point across! And to get that point, we need to understand this word in the Greek language—the language of John's day.

Believe (*pisteú*☐): You're probably familiar with the fact that the Greeks had several words for *love*, while the English language has only one. We *love* our family, we *love* good pizza, and we *love* a certain movie—and no matter what degree of intensity we feel, we use the same word to express it.

The word *believe*, however, works the opposite way. In English, we have many words for *believe* ("I believe," "I think," "I know," for example), but this isn't so in the Greek language. When Greek writers wanted to express belief, trust, or certainty to any degree, they used *pisteú*☐. Consequently, this word was loaded with meaning—and it was expected that your life (your behavior, attitudes, and character) would be driven by that belief. What good is it to *believe* in something (or Someone) if that belief doesn't affect your behavior? In addition, John was very emphatic about what (or whom) we're to *believe in*. The only way to eternal life is belief that Jesus is the Christ, the Son of God.

By the way, believers today often make a misguided distinction between the words *belief* and *faith*, thinking one of these words indicates a higher level of faith or even a saving level of faith. But the Bible makes no distinction. Both the verb form (*to believe*) and the noun form (*faith*) are related to the same Greek word, *pisteú*☐. Knowing this will help you keep the discussion on track if students start debating the difference between belief and faith.

---

2 For those who get into this sort of stuff, various forms of *believe* (believing, belief, believed, and so on) occur 75 times in John, while only nine times in Matthew, 15 in Mark, and 10 in Luke. These counts are based on the New International Version of Scripture.

Digging Deeper

True Belief

Now that we're armed with some background on this key word, let's dig a little deeper.

Three passages from John are printed on your Scripture sheet. As you read these passages, do a couple of things:

1. Look for the word *believe* and mark it uniquely. (You might draw a light bulb ![light bulb] each time the word or a form of it appears.) Keep in mind the definition of the word *believe*.

2. Look for any benefits of believing (mark a "smiley" ![smiley] over these), as well as any consequences of not believing (a "frowny" face ![frowny] will do).

When you've finished marking the passages, list below what you discovered about the benefits of believing and the consequences of not believing.

Benefits of Believing	Consequences of Not Believing

You should note one final observation before we move on. Spend a couple of minutes meditating on John 3:21. Read it two or three times. Did you notice Jesus doesn't use the word *believe* here, but uses a phrase that actually *defines* the kind of belief and behavior he's looking for? Write that phrase below. Think about how it relates to the kind of believing—letting your belief drive your actions—we're considering here.

One more thing: According to verse 21, what happens when we live by the truth?

Taking It Inward

Eternal Life. So What?

Have you ever had a moment when something—like a favorite hobby or sport—suddenly "got in your blood"? When that happens, we go from being casual onlookers to motivated participants. Do you get the feeling that this is what John hoped would happen in his readers' lives? Take a few moments to prayerfully complete these exercises:

> Look over your "Benefits of Believing" list above. In the space here, write a benefit that makes you go, "Wow!" Then write a sentence or two praising God for this benefit.

> Look at your "Consequences of Not Believing" list. Do you have friends or family members who are in danger of experiencing these consequences? Pause to pray for them as you list their names here.

> Is the prospect of eternal life a motivator for you, or is it too far off? What needs to change for eternal life to become more of a motivator?

> What changes do you need to make so your lifestyle can be defined as "living by the truth"?

> The big question: What difference has the presence of Jesus Christ made in your life? Does your lifestyle (outlook, personality, habits, attitudes toward people) reflect the fact that you are a child "born of God" (John 1:12-13) and have begun living an "eternal life" (John 3:16)? If so, in what ways? If not, why not?

Wrapping It Up

Use the session outlines that follow this Prep It to select the appropriate Teach It guide for your session based on the age of your students and the setting of your session (full Teach It guides are on the CD-ROM accompanying this book). The instructions in the front of this book contain descriptions of each guide. Then read through the guide so you're familiar with the flow of the session and confident with each exercise. Be sure to allow time for printing or photocopying student pages, pulling together any other materials needed (see the Materials step in the Teach It guide), and hole-punching student pages for their three-ring notebooks.

John made it a point to record Jesus' miracles, signs, wonders, and teachings so the world would *believe* and enjoy *eternal life*! Pray for your students—that their hearts will be open to *believing* in Jesus in the way John describes and that they'll live in a way that shows they trust in him as the very Son of God. Pray that your life and your students' lives will be a record of the miracles, signs, wonders, and teachings of Jesus, so the people around you will also believe and experience eternal life.

WEB SUPPORT:
Remember to check out Web support for *See, Believe, Live* at www.inword.org. You'll find updated media suggestions (music, video clips), along with additional prep helps and even more application ideas. When at www.inword.org, look for the Digging Deeper series icon. You'll find password information in the Instructions at the front of this book.

Digging In

Purpose Statement

John 20:30-31

30 Jesus did many other miraculous signs in the presence of his disciples, which are not recorded in this book.

31 But these are written that you may believe that Jesus is the Christ, the Son of God, and that by believing you may have life in his name.

Digging Deeper

True Belief

John 1:6-13

6   There came a man who was sent from God; his name was John.

7   He came as a witness to testify concerning that light, so that through him all men might believe.

8   He himself was not the light; he came only as a witness to the light.

9   The true light that gives light to every man was coming into the world.

10   He was in the world, and though the world was made through him, the world did not recognize him.

11   He came to that which was his own, but his own did not receive him.

12   Yet to all who received him, to those who believed in his name, he gave the right to become children of God—

13   children born not of natural descent, nor of human decision or a husband's will, but born of God.

John 3:11-21
(Jesus is speaking.)

11 "I tell you the truth, we speak of what we know, and we testify to what we have seen, but still you people do not accept our testimony.

12 I have spoken to you of earthly things and you do not believe; how then will you believe if I speak of heavenly things?

13 No one has ever gone into heaven except the one who came from heaven—the Son of Man.

14 Just as Moses lifted up the snake in the desert, so the Son of Man must be lifted up,

15 that everyone who believes in him may have eternal life.

16 For God so loved the world that he gave his one and only Son, that whoever believes in him shall not perish but have eternal life.

17 For God did not send his Son into the world to condemn the world, but to save the world through him.

18 Whoever believes in him is not condemned, but whoever does not believe stands condemned already because he has not believed in the name of God's one and only Son.

19 This is the verdict: Light has come into the world, but men loved darkness instead of light because their deeds were evil.

20 Everyone who does evil hates the light, and will not come into the light for fear that his deeds will be exposed.

21 But whoever lives by the truth comes into the light, so that it may be seen plainly that what he has done has been done through God."

ONE WEEK OUT

Remind and encourage your students about the study.

1. Materials

For this session each student will need—
- the Session 1 Scripture sheet
- the student journal page for Session 1
- a three-ring notebook in which to keep his or her Scripture sheets and journal pages over the course of the study
- his or her own Bible and a pen

You'll also need—
- a pack of colored pencils (at least two colors per student)
- a wall-size Scripture sheet of John 20:30-31 (data projection onto paper or poster board, a giant printout from Kinko's, or a handmade poster)
- colored large-tip markers or Sharpie pens
- a favorite book (one you read recently or as a teenager; it doesn't have to be a Christian book)
- optional: marshmallows

2. Session Intro

GOALS OF SESSION 1

As students experience this session, they will—
- discover John's purpose in writing his Gospel.
- be introduced to the connection between *true belief* and a changed life.
- be challenged to become a "sign" that will point others to belief in Jesus.

PRAYER

OPEN: *BOOK BACKGROUND*
Use one of your favorite books to introduce the idea of studying a book of the Bible.

3. Digging In: *Purpose Statement*

Group Dig: Explore John 20:30-31 to discover the reason why John wrote his Gospel.

4. Digging Deeper: *True Belief*

Group Interaction: Talk about the Greeks' use of the word *believe*, and then test-drive this word by reading and responding to John 3:14-18 interactively.

5. Taking It Inward: *Eternal Life. So What?*

Personal Retreat: Apply the benefits of believing to everyday life.

6. Wrapping It Up: *Bumper-Sticker Theology*

Create a bumper-sticker phrase or text message to summarize the main challenge in this session.

ONE WEEK OUT

Remind and encourage your students about the study.

1. Materials

For this session each student will need—
- the Session 1 Scripture sheet
- the student journal page for Session 1
- a three-ring notebook in which to keep his or her Scripture sheets and journal pages over the course of the study
- his or her own Bible and a pen

You'll also need—
- a whiteboard and markers
- a pack of colored pencils (at least two colors per student)
- a wall-size Scripture sheet of John 20:30-31 (data projection onto paper or poster board, a giant printout from Kinko's, or a handmade poster)
- colored large-tip markers or Sharpie pens
- a favorite book (one you read recently or as a teenager; it doesn't have to be a Christian book)

2. Session Intro

GOALS OF SESSION 1

As students experience this session, they will—
- discover John's purpose in writing his Gospel.
- be introduced to the connection between *true belief* and a changed life.
- be challenged to become a "sign" that will point others to belief in Jesus.

PRAYER

OPEN: *BOOK BACKGROUND*
Use one of your favorite books to introduce the idea of studying a book of the Bible.

3. Digging In: *Purpose Statement*

Group Dig: Explore key passages to discover the reason why John wrote his Gospel.

4. Digging Deeper: *True Belief*

Group Interaction: Talk about the Greeks' use of the word *believe*. Then test-drive this word in John 3:14-18.

5. Taking It Inward: *Eternal Life. So What?*

Personal Retreat: Apply the benefits of believing to everyday life.

6. Wrapping It Up: *Bumper-Sticker Theology*

Create a bumper-sticker phrase or text message to summarize the main challenge in this session.

ONE WEEK OUT

Remind and encourage your students about the study.

1. Materials

For this session each student will need—
- the Session 1 Scripture sheet
- the student journal page for Session 1
- a three-ring notebook in which to keep his or her Scripture sheets and journal pages over the course of the study
- his or her own Bible and a pen

You'll also need—
- a whiteboard and markers
- a pack of colored pencils (at least two colors per student)
- a favorite book (one you read recently or as a teenager; it doesn't have to be a Christian book)

2. Session Intro

GOALS OF SESSION 1
As students experience this session, they will—
- discover John's purpose in writing his Gospel.
- be introduced to the connection between *true belief* and a changed life.
- be challenged to become a "sign" that will point others to belief in Jesus.

PRAYER

OPEN: *BOOK BACKGROUND*
Use one of your favorite books to introduce the idea of studying a book of the Bible.

3. Digging In: *Purpose Statement*

Group Dig: Explore key passages to discover the reason why John wrote his Gospel.

4. Digging Deeper: *True Belief*

Group Dig: Talk about the Greeks' use of the word *believe*. Then test-drive this word in John 3:11-18.

5. Taking It Inward: *Eternal Life. So What?*

Personal Retreat: Apply the benefits of believing to everyday life.

6. Wrapping It Up: *T-Shirt Theology*

Create a T-shirt phrase or text message to summarize the main challenge in this session.

ONE WEEK OUT

Remind and encourage your students about the study.

1. Materials

For this session each student will need—
- the Session 1 Scripture sheet
- the student journal page for Session 1
- a three-ring notebook in which to keep his or her Scripture sheets and journal pages over the course of the study
- his or her own Bible and a pen

You'll also need—
- a whiteboard and markers
- a pack of colored pencils (at least two colors per student)

2. Session Intro

GOALS OF SESSION 1

As students experience this session, they will—
- discover John's purpose in writing his Gospel.
- be introduced to the connection between *true belief* and a changed life.
- be challenged to become a "sign" that will point others to belief in Jesus.

PRAYER

OPEN: *BOOK BACKGROUND*
Group Interaction: Have students talk about their favorite books to introduce the idea of studying a book of the Bible.

3. Digging In: *Purpose Statement*

Group Dig: Explore key passages to discover the purpose behind the Gospel of John.

4. Digging Deeper: *True Belief*

Group Dig: Talk about the Greeks' use of the word *believe*. Then test-drive this word in John 3:11-18.

5. Taking It Inward: *Eternal Life. So What?*

Personal Retreat: Journal about ways to apply the benefits of believing to everyday life.

6. Wrapping It Up: *Sharing and Prayer*

Share and pray with a partner, or conclude with large-group prayer.

ONE WEEK OUT

Remind and encourage your students about the study.

1. Materials

For this session each student will need—
- his or her own Bible
- optional: the student journal page for Session 1 (Using the student journal page is optional in the coffeehouse setting since table space will be limited.)

You'll also need—
- a pack of pencils with erasers
- optional: a few spare Bibles for students who've forgotten theirs

2. Session Intro

GOALS OF SESSION 1
As students experience this session, they will—
- discover John's purpose in writing his Gospel.
- be introduced to the connection between *true belief* and a changed life.
- be challenged to become a "sign" that will point others to belief in Jesus.

PRAYER

OPEN: *BOOK BACKGROUND*
Group Interaction: Have students talk about their favorite books to introduce the idea of studying a book of the Bible.

3. Digging In: *Purpose Statement*

Group Study: Explore key passages to discover the purpose behind the Gospel of John.

4. Digging Deeper: *True Belief*

Group Dig: Talk about the Greeks' use of the word *believe*. Then test-drive this word in John 3:11-18.

5. Taking It Inward: *Eternal Life. So What?*

Personal Sharing: Apply the benefits of believing to everyday life.

6. Wrapping It Up: *Bumper-Sticker Theology*

Create a bumper-sticker phrase or text message to summarize the main challenge in this session.

1. Materials (Optional)

- Movie Clip: *Indiana Jones and the Last Crusade*. Scene: Indiana Jones is to "step out" in faith across a huge chasm (Chapter 33—counter cues, 1:47:00 to 1:49:00).
- Images from a Web search of "The Great Blondin"
- Play-Doh (or something else crafty like pipe cleaners) for an impromptu art creation during the talk

2. Optional Opens

Movie Clip: *Indiana Jones and the Last Crusade*
Story: the Great Blondin over Niagara Falls
Visual/Interactive: belief in something you don't understand
Personal Story: a time you took a risk and really benefited

3. Digging In

John 1:10-13
Personal Story: Share about a time you struggled to submit to something you didn't understand.
God's Perspective: what it looks like when we ignore him and fail to believe
optional Play-Doh illustration

4. Taking It Inward

Jeremiah 2:13
Repeat John 1:12-13
John 20:31 (John's purpose statement)

- What the Bible means by *believe* (the Greek word *pisteú*☐)
- True belief is more than a simple acknowledgement. True belief shows up in our actions.
- A challenge to believe

SESSION 2

Setting the Heart

Each Gospel writer began his account of Jesus' life in his own way. Perhaps when John sat down to put his "memoirs" to papyrus and ink, he decided to go for something unique. Maybe he thought people had had enough of long genealogies (Matthew) and orderly accounts (Luke). It was time to put it all together—theology, philosophy, history—in an expressive way that explained the "Good News," telling us *who* Jesus is and *why* belief in him is so important.

Take a moment to prepare your heart to experience one of the most poetic passages in all of Scripture—John 1—by reading what Paul wrote about the power of this "Good News," a message that carries the power of life and death.

> All of us also lived among [the Gentiles] at one time, gratifying the cravings of our sinful nature and following its desires and thoughts. Like the rest, we were by nature objects of wrath. But because of his great love for us, God, who is rich in mercy, made us alive with Christ even when we were dead in transgressions—it is by grace you have been saved. (Ephesians 2:3-5)

Digging In

The Word on the Word

You may have heard Matthew, Mark, and Luke collectively called the *synoptic* Gospels, *synoptic* meaning "to see the whole together." These three Gospels are similar in their scope and presentation of Jesus, while John's Gospel stands alone. John didn't record many of the events the writers of the synoptic Gospels recorded—and John recorded many events that are unique to his Gospel and not found in the other three. But the most telling differences between John's Gospel and the others are his interpretations of Jesus' ministry and his expressive use of the Greek language. The world was beginning to develop theories about who Jesus was, theories that were creating gray areas with regard to following Jesus. John is very clear that there is no gray when it comes to who Jesus is—it's either black or white, light or dark.

Using your Scripture sheet, read John 1:1-18.

As you read, mark every mention of Jesus with a cross. ✝ Be sure to include words that refer to Jesus, such as *he, him, light, Word,* and *life.* See if you can discern what John is stressing about Jesus.

After you've read and marked the passage, list below everything you learn about Jesus as "Word." Then list what you learn about Jesus as "light."

Jesus as Word	Jesus as Light

In these two lists, you now have a fairly comprehensive description of Jesus. Meditate on these truths, bearing in mind that when John wrote his Gospel, many errant theories about Jesus were floating around. (Sound familiar?) Based on what John said about Jesus, what do you think the world believed about him at the time of John's writing?

Digging Deeper

Sharper Image

God has been working a plan involving Jesus since before creation. Now we get to experience all of God's plan through his Son—a plan that includes a very specific beneficiary...*you!*

The chart below is a timeline on which to depict your spiritual journey, as told by God's Word. The cross represents the time when you accepted ("believed," to use John's word) Jesus as the Christ, the Son of the living God.

Read from your Bible the three passages noted below, and place the following details in the appropriate column on the timeline.

1. Everything you learn about "you" (look for words such as *us, we,* and *you) before* Jesus was a part of your life.

2. Everything you learn about "you" *since* Jesus has become a part of your life.

Colossians 1:13-18

1 Peter 1:17-25

John 1:1-7

As you write this info below, personalize it with first-person pronouns such as *me, I,* or *my.* Keep your eyes peeled for anything about Jesus that parallels what you observed in John 1. Bear in mind that these passages come from letters written by Paul, Peter, and John (yep, the same John who wrote the Gospel)—three men God used in mighty ways to spread his Word just after Jesus' ministry on earth.

What I Learn About Me

Before Jesus	Since Jesus
Colossians 1:13-18	**Colossians 1:13-18**
1 Peter 1:17-25	**1 Peter 1:17-25**
1 John 1:1-7	**1 John 1:1-7**

Take a minute to prayerfully meditate on the facts you've listed in each column. Let God speak to you about your life before and after Christ became part of it.

Now reread the items to the right of the cross. These are things of which you, as a believer, can take full advantage. But here's the question: *How does knowing about these things affect your daily life?* Printed below are several scenarios. Journal in the space provided your thoughts about how these scriptures (including John 1) can impact your behavior in these situations:

Dealing with temptation...

Feeling guilty over mistakes you've made...

Interacting with people who aren't friendly to the Christian faith...

Overcoming difficult circumstances, such as disease or tragedy...

Letting your life be a witness to the light (as John the Baptist was in John 1)...

Wrapping It Up

Truth in Action

Review everything you've discovered in Scripture about Jesus during this Prep It. Look over the crosses you marked in Scripture and the notes you've made in the pages above. In the space below, write at least two things God is saying to you personally about his Son.

1.

2.

Now read over everything you've discovered about yourself from the Digging Deeper exercise above. Write at least two truths that can motivate you to take some kind of action (adjust an attitude, change a habit) or that can impact your outlook on life.

    1.

    2.

Finally, grab a cup of coffee, find a comfy chair, and reread John 1 from your Scripture sheet. As you read, listen for the answers to these questions:

    What is John saying to me about the man with whom he was privileged to walk?

    What difference does Jesus make in my life?

Select the appropriate Teach It guide for your session (full Teach It guides are on the CD-ROM accompanying this book). Then read through the guide so you're familiar with the flow of the session and confident with each exercise. Be sure to allow time for printing or photocopying student pages and pulling together any materials needed (see the Materials step in the Teach It guide).

Here's your last "prep" exercise: Spend some time praying for your students, that their hearts will be changed by what God says about Jesus and them.

Bonus Round

John 1 covers more ground than we're dealing with in this session, so you may want to do the following exercise to acquaint yourself with the portion of John 1 this lesson doesn't cover. This exercise isn't included in any of the Teach It guides, but feel free to create your own for your students to do on their own or as part of your session if time allows.

Titles of Jesus

Read John 1:19-51, looking for any titles given to Jesus. Record these on a separate piece of paper. Next, choose one title and spend some time with Jesus as that title. Here's an example:

Title: "Lamb of God"—John 1:29, 36

To Experience Jesus as the Lamb of God:

Using an exhaustive Bible concordance or Bible software, find other references to Jesus as the Lamb of God. For example:

Isaiah 53:7

1 Corinthians 5:7

1 Peter 1:18-19

Revelation 7:14-17

Meditate on these passages, journaling anything God brings to mind regarding Jesus as the Lamb.

How can you adjust your walk with God in a way that acknowledges Jesus as the Lamb of God?

WEB SUPPORT:
Remember to check out Web support for *See, Believe, Live* at www.inword.org You'll find updated media suggestions (music, video clips), along with additional prep helps and even more application ideas. When at www.inword.org look for the Digging Deeper series icon. You'll find password information in the Instructions at the front of this book.

John 1:1-18

1 In the beginning was the Word, and the Word was with God, and the Word was God.

2 He was with God in the beginning.

3 Through him all things were made; without him nothing was made that has been made.

4 In him was life, and that life was the light of men.

5 The light shines in the darkness, but the darkness has not understood it.

6 There came a man who was sent from God; his name was John.

7 He came as a witness to testify concerning that light, so that through him all men might believe.

8 He himself was not the light; he came only as a witness to the light.

9 The true light that gives light to every man was coming into the world.

10 He was in the world, and though the world was made through him, the world did not recognize him.

11 He came to that which was his own, but his own did not receive him.

12 Yet to all who received him, to those who believed in his name, he gave the right to become children of God—

13 children born not of natural descent, nor of human decision or a husband's will, but born of God.

14 The Word became flesh and made his dwelling among us. We have seen his glory, the glory of the One and Only, who came from the Father, full of grace and truth.

15 John testifies concerning him. He cries out, saying, "This was he of whom I said, 'He who comes after me has surpassed me because he was before me.'"

16 From the fullness of his grace we have all received one blessing after another.

17 For the law was given through Moses; grace and truth came through Jesus Christ.

18 No one has ever seen God, but God the One and Only, who is at the Father's side, has made him known.

1. Materials

For this session each student will need—
- the Session 2 Scripture sheet
- the student journal page for Session 2
- his or her own Bible, a pen, and a notebook

You'll also need—
- a whiteboard and markers
- a pack of colored pencils (at least two colors per student)
- various images of Jesus to print and/or project; collect these prior to your session by searching Google Images. Variety is the key; make sure you include as many different art mediums as you possibly can (e.g., stained glass, wood carving, cartoon, oil on canvas, etc.). Include both flattering and unflattering images.

2. Session Intro

GOALS OF SESSION 2

As students experience this session, they will—
- be strengthened in their belief in Jesus, based on truths in John 1.
- learn how to break away the "spiritual crust" that can form when we have an under-used, out-of-date picture of Jesus.
- be challenged to personalize the historic, worldwide impact of Jesus' existence.

PRAYER

OPEN: *EVERY PICTURE TELLS A STORY*
Look at various artists' renderings of Jesus and think about what each one says about each artist's preconceived notions of Jesus.

3. Digging In: *The Word on the Word*

Group Dig: Explore John 1:1-18 to experience Jesus as Word and Light.

4. Digging Deeper: *Sharper Image*

Personal Retreat: Understand how knowledge of the Word and Light impacts our everyday situations.

5. Wrapping It Up: *Truth in Action*

Lock into simple truths that can enhance our image of Jesus and change our daily living.

JOHN 1
"IN THE BEGINNING..."

1. Materials

For this session each student will need—
- the Session 2 Scripture sheet
- the student journal page for Session 2
- his or her own Bible, a pen, and a notebook

You'll also need—
- a whiteboard and markers
- a pack of colored pencils (at least two colors per student)
- various images of Jesus to project or print; find these by using a search engine such as Google Images. Select flattering and at least one not-so-flattering image for variety.

2. Session Intro

GOALS OF SESSION 2
As students experience this session, they will—
- be strengthened in their belief in Jesus, based on truths in John 1.
- learn how to break through the "spiritual crust" that forms when we have an under-used, out-of-date picture of Jesus.
- be challenged to personalize the historic, worldwide impact of Jesus' existence.

PRAYER

OPEN: *EVERY PICTURE TELLS A STORY*
Look at various artists' renderings of Jesus and think about what each one says about each artist's preconceived notions of Jesus.

3. Digging In: *The Word on the Word*

Group Dig: Explore John 1:1-18 to experience Jesus as Word and Light.

4. Digging Deeper: *Sharper Image*

Personal Retreat: Understand how knowledge of the Word and Light impacts our everyday situations.

5. Wrapping It Up: *Truth in Action*

Lock into simple truths that can enhance our image of Jesus and change our daily living.

1. Materials

For this session each student will need—
- the Session 2 Scripture sheet
- the student journal page for Session 2
- his or her own Bible, a pen, and a notebook

You'll also need—
- a whiteboard and markers
- a pack of colored pencils (at least two colors per student)
- various images of Jesus to project or print; find these by searching Google Images. Select flattering and at least one not-so-flattering image for variety.

2. Session Intro

GOALS OF SESSION 2
As students experience this session, they will—
- be strengthened in their belief in Jesus, based on truths in John 1.
- learn how to break through the "spiritual crust" that forms when we have an under-used, out-of-date picture of Jesus.
- be challenged to personalize the historic, worldwide impact of Jesus' existence.

PRAYER

OPEN: *EVERY PICTURE TELLS A STORY*
Look at various artists' renderings of Jesus and think about what each one says about each artist's preconceived notions of Jesus.

3. Digging In: *The Word on the Word*
Group Dig: Explore John 1:1-18 to experience Jesus as Word and Light.

4. Digging Deeper: *Sharper Image*
Personal Retreat: Understand how knowledge of the Word and Light impacts our everyday situations.
Group Interaction (optional): Apply this knowledge in a role-play exercise by helping a "friend" through some everyday situations.

5. Wrapping It Up: *Truth in Action*
Lock into simple truths that can enhance our image of Jesus and change our daily living.

1. Materials

For this session each student will need—
- the Session 2 Scripture sheet
- the student journal page for Session 2
- his or her own Bible, a pen, and a notebook

You'll also need—
- a whiteboard and markers
- a pack of colored pencils (at least two colors per student)

2. Session Intro

GOALS OF SESSION 2

As students experience this session, they will—
- be strengthened in their belief in Jesus, based on truths in John 1.
- learn how to break through the "spiritual crust" that forms when we have an under-used, out-of-date picture of Jesus.
- be challenged to personalize the historic, worldwide impact of Jesus' existence.

PRAYER

OPEN: *EVERY PICTURE TELLS A STORY*
Look at various artists' renderings of Jesus and think about what each one says about each artist's preconceived notions of Jesus.

3. Digging In: *The Word on the Word*

Group Dig: Explore John 1:1-18 to experience Jesus as Word and Light.

4. Digging Deeper: *Sharper Image*

Personal Retreat: Understand how knowledge of the Word and Light impacts our everyday situations.

5. Wrapping It Up: *Truth in Action*

Lock into simple truths that can enhance our image of Jesus and change our daily living.

1. Materials

For this session each student will need—
- his or her own Bible
- optional: the student journal page for Session 2 (Using the student journal page is optional in the coffeehouse setting since table space will be limited.)

You'll also need—
- a pack of pencils with erasers
- optional: a few spare Bibles for students who've forgotten theirs

2. Session Intro

GOALS OF SESSION 2

As students experience this session, they will—
- be strengthened in their belief in Jesus, based on truths in John 1.
- learn how to break through the "spiritual crust" that forms when we have an under-used, out-of-date picture of Jesus.
- be challenged to personalize the historic, worldwide impact of Jesus' existence.

PRAYER

OPEN: *EVERY PICTURE TELLS A STORY*
Group Interaction: Discuss the different mental pictures of Jesus that people carry around.

3. Digging In: *The Word on the Word*

Group Dig: Explore John 1:1-18 to experience Jesus as Word and Light.

4. Digging Deeper: *Sharper Image*

Group Dig: Understand how knowledge of the Word and Light impacts our everyday situations.

5. Wrapping It Up: *Truth in Action*

Lock into simple truths that can enhance our image of Jesus and change our daily living.

1. Materials (Optional)

- Movie Trailer: *Charlie and the Chocolate Factory.* Play the trailer from the DVD, or search for it on a video-sharing Web site such as YouTube.
- Some simple lighting effects in the room where you meet, such as: darkness (as dark as possible), minimal light (flashlight), full light (all available room lights, stage lights, or even a light show)

2. Optional Opens

Visual Illustration: movie trailer from *Charlie and the Chocolate Factory*
Story: Tell of a time you received something you didn't deserve.

3. Digging In

John 1:6-13

- Explain who John the Baptist was.
- Point out what John understood about Jesus—and about himself.

4. Taking It Inward

Visual Illustration: changing the room from dark to light, illustrating our lives before, during, and after Jesus.

5. Wrapping It Up

Challenge students to think about what "state of Jesus" they're in—before, during, or after.

SESSION 3

Setting the Heart

Ever notice how easily a church or ministry can turn *anything* into a lifeless ritual? That's not a cynical question, but an observation of a very real human tendency. Even the sacred act of communion can become an activity that simply gets slotted into a busy worship experience. All we see is a wafer and a cup—not a broken body and blood. In his infinite wisdom, God knew his people could easily slip from genuine spirituality into pseudo-spirituality—a spirituality defined by busy religious activities but with little or no heart connection. Perhaps that's why he inspired John to record a conversation between Jesus and Nicodemus. There was Nicodemus, a leader of the Pharisees, history's most renowned pseudo-religious group that wrote the book on meaningless religious activity, talking with Jesus, history's most renowned authority on *true* spirituality.

Anything that is *not* God can become a substitute for God—even *good* things. Maybe that's why the first of the Ten Commandments gives stern warning against this. As you read this commandment below, instead of picturing obvious "other gods," such as Buddha or pride or TV, think about the more subtle things Christians substitute for a personal walk with God, things that seem good—like church activities, ministry involvement, religious programs—but may not actually connect us to God.

> You shall have no other gods before me. You shall not make for yourself an idol in the form of anything in heaven above or on the earth beneath or in the waters below. (Exodus 20:3-4)

Digging In

Nic at Night

How ironic that it was a secret meeting between Jesus and a discreet Pharisee that generated the most famous Bible verse of all time, John 3:16. For the next few minutes, listen to Jesus' words through the ears of his audience of one—a man concerned with seeking entry into God's kingdom through visible, tangible ways—ways that could easily become idols.

Read John 3:1-11 using your Scripture sheet. As you read, do the following:

1. Use a special color or symbol to mark every mention of Nicodemus, such as a stick man or the Star of David .

2. Carefully read Jesus' responses to Nicodemus. As you do, mark the words *born* and *birth* wherever they occur.

Now record below everything you learn about Nicodemus. Then list everything Jesus taught him about spiritual birth.

Nicodemus	Spiritual Birth

Insight

Nicodemus Sightings

Nicodemus makes three appearances in John's Gospel—the only Gospel that mentions him. You'll gain further insight on Nicodemus by reading the other two scenes where he appears. Read the verses below from your Bible, asking yourself: *What's going on? Who's involved? What is Nicodemus doing?*

John 7:43-53   John 19:38-42

Based on what you've read, did Jesus' words in John 3 have any impact on Nicodemus? As best you can, back up your answer from Scripture.

Now write a thought or two noting the difference between Nicodemus' first visit with Jesus and his last.

Insight

A Little Greek

The Greek word translated "again" (an[]then), as in "born again," can also be translated "from above" (see John 3:31 and 19:11). In Jesus' day, this word meant "anew" or "from the beginning."[3] The fact that Nicodemus thought Jesus was referring to reentering his mother's womb indicates that he understood Jesus to mean "again."

In his Gospel, John uses the word an[]then to convey a strong tie to the supernatural—a birth that is in no way linked to anything on earth. Thus, Jesus was describing a transformation that can only be explained as "starting from above." This info may refresh your understanding of the phrase *born again*, which has become something of a cultural cliché—even a political lightning rod—in our day.

Digging Deeper

Belief Benefits

Let's look at Jesus' response to Nicodemus. Read John 3:10-21 using your Scripture sheet. As you read, mark the word *believe* (and any similar phrases) in a unique way, maybe with a light bulb 💡 .

When you've finished, look at the words and phrases surrounding the word *believe*. Draw some contrasts between nonbelievers and believers, and write your thoughts below.

Nonbelievers	Believers

CROSS-CHECKING

Do Over

Before we apply what God is showing us, let's look at some other verses that teach about spiritual birth. Read the passages below from your Bible. Record beneath the verse references what you learn about spiritual birth.

John 1:10-13

---

3 Paul R. McReynolds, ed., *Word Study Greek-English New Testament* (Wheaton: Tyndale House, 1998) and Leon Morris, The Gospel According to John, *The New International Commentary on the New Testament* (Grand Rapids: Eerdmans Publishing, 1995).

Titus 3:4-7

1 Peter 1:22-25

Taking It Inward

A New Kind of Birthday

Considering what being "born again" entails, do you get the feeling God is looking for more from us than a "decision for Christ" after weighing the facts? More than simply giving the right answers to a set of simple questions about where we'll "spend eternity"? More than our getting involved in religious activities? Spiritual rebirth is total transformation—and it has nothing to do with anything on earth. It comes from above. Let the following questions prompt your thoughts as you meditate on these things.

1. Looking over all the info you've recorded on spiritual birth, circle the things that *must happen* in order for you to see the kingdom of God. What is God telling you about *your* spiritual birth?

2. What words or phrases do John, Titus, and Peter use to describe the process of spiritual birth?

John _____

Titus _____

Peter _____

3. What connection do you see between Nicodemus' background and how Jesus responded to his question?

4. We tend to be like Nicodemus in many ways, defining our spiritual lives by tangible or practical things we can see, touch, and do. List below any tangible/practical things in your life that are at risk of defining your spiritual life.

What is Jesus saying to you through the Scriptures about these things?

5. If a person is truly born again through belief in Jesus Christ, there will be a transformation in his or her behavior. As we've already seen, belief and behavior are inseparable. Jesus gave a great definition for what it means to believe in John 3:21; the New American Standard version reads, "But he who *practices the truth* comes to the Light…" (emphasis mine). Think for a minute about the phrase *practices the truth*. What does that look like? What does "practice the truth" mean to you? Jot your thoughts in the space below.

Are you *practicing the truth*? Has your rebirth compelled you to *practice the truth*?

6. Look again at John 1:10-13. If you've been born again, you have two birthdays—a physical birthday and a spiritual birthday. According to these verses, which birthday is more important? Have you ever celebrated your "spiritual birthday"? Would you like to?

WEB SUPPORT:
Remember to check out Web support for *See, Believe, Live* at www. inword.org. You'll find updated media suggestions (music, video clips), along with additional prep helps and even more application ideas. When at www.inword.org, look for the Digging Deeper series icon. You'll find password information in the Instructions at the front of this book.

Wrapping It Up

It's Party Time!

Select the appropriate Teach It guide for your session (full Teach It guides are on the CD-ROM accompanying this book). Then read through the guide so you're familiar with the flow of the session and confident with each exercise. Be sure to allow time for printing or photocopying student pages and pulling together any materials needed (see the Materials step in the Teach It guide).

Before your group meets, think seriously about the closing exercise in the Teach It guide. You may want to close the session by planning or throwing a spiritual birthday bash!

Application of this study is totally personal—no challenges to impact a school campus, head off to do missions in Africa, or give away all your worldly possessions. This scene between Nicodemus and Jesus goes right to the heart of what it means to be a Christian. It's a transformation that's so radical it requires a new starting point—a rebirth. The goal of this session is to help your students evaluate their personal belief in Jesus and allow themselves to be born from above. They should also see that spiritual rebirth places them in an entirely new realm—the kingdom of God, which operates on a different time clock from the physical world. Their eternal life has begun! Therefore, their spiritual birthdays should take precedence over their physical birthdays.

John 3:1-21

1 Now there was a man of the Pharisees named Nicodemus, a member of the Jewish ruling council.

2 He came to Jesus at night and said, "Rabbi, we know you are a teacher who has come from God. For no one could perform the miraculous signs you are doing if God were not with him."

3 In reply Jesus declared, "I tell you the truth, no one can see the kingdom of God unless he is born again."

4 "How can a man be born when he is old?" Nicodemus asked. "Surely he cannot enter a second time into his mother's womb to be born!"

5 Jesus answered, "I tell you the truth, no one can enter the kingdom of God unless he is born of water and the Spirit.

6 Flesh gives birth to flesh, but the Spirit gives birth to spirit.

7 You should not be surprised at my saying, 'You must be born again.'

8 The wind blows wherever it pleases. You hear its sound, but you cannot tell where it comes from or where it is going. So it is with everyone born of the Spirit."

9 "How can this be?" Nicodemus asked.

10 "You are Israel's teacher," said Jesus, "and do you not understand these things?

11 I tell you the truth, we speak of what we know, and we testify to what we have seen, but still you people do not accept our testimony.

12 I have spoken to you of earthly things and you do not believe; how then will you believe if I speak of heavenly things?

13 No one has ever gone into heaven except the one who came from heaven—the Son of Man.

14 Just as Moses lifted up the snake in the desert, so the Son of Man must be lifted up,

15 that everyone who believes in him may have eternal life.

16 For God so loved the world that he gave his one and only Son, that whoever believes in him shall not perish but have eternal life.

17 For God did not send his Son into the world to condemn the world, but to save the world through him.

18 Whoever believes in him is not condemned, but whoever does not believe stands condemned already because he has not believed in the name of God's one and only Son.

19 This is the verdict: Light has come into the world, but men loved darkness instead of light because their deeds were evil.

20 Everyone who does evil hates the light, and will not come into the light for fear that his deeds will be exposed.

21 But whoever lives by the truth comes into the light, so that it may be seen plainly that what he has done has been done through God."

1. Materials

For this session each student will need—
- the Session 3 Scripture sheet
- the student journal page for Session 3
- his or her own Bible, a pen, and a notebook

You'll also need—
- a whiteboard and markers
- a pack of colored pencils (at least two colors per student)
- picture sets of butterflies, frogs, ladybugs, dragonflies, and their corresponding larvae that you have Googled and printed out beforehand. Throw in some robot/vehicle picture sets from the movie *Transformers* for fun.
- optional: music for the Transformer exercise (something fun or light to serve as "musical chairs"-type music)
- optional: prizes for the first two students to have a correct match
- optional: a large cake and several tubes of icing (one for every two or three students). You may want to write "Happy Birthlife!" in icing on the cake.
- optional: cupcakes, markers, and a paper plate for each student

2. Session Intro

GOALS OF SESSION 3

As students experience this session, they will—
- gain a true understanding (as opposed to a cliché understanding) of the phrase *born again*.
- make a connection between their spiritual birth and God's eternal time clock.
- be invited to acknowledge their spiritual birth in a unique way.

PRAYER

OPEN: *TRANSFORMER*

Use images of metamorphosis—such as frogs and Transformers—to illustrate total change.

3. Digging In: *Nic at Night*

Group Dig: Explore the dynamics of Nic's clandestine meeting with Jesus.

4. Insight: *Deep Background*

Provide general background on the Pharisees, personal background on Nicodemus, and historic background on the phrase *born again*.

5. Digging Deeper: *Belief Benefits*

Group Dig: Discover that believing has its privileges.

6. Cross-Checking: *Do Over*

Personal Retreat: Breathe new life into the phrase *born again* by seeing how our days can change when we take new birth seriously.

7. Taking It Inward: *A New Kind of Birthday*

Group Interaction: Discuss which of our two birthdays is more important.

8. Wrapping It Up: *It's Party Time!*

Group Interaction: Throw a "Happy Birthlife!" party!

1. Materials

For this session each student will need—
- the Session 3 Scripture sheet
- the student journal page for Session 3
- his or her own Bible, a pen, and a notebook

You'll also need—
- a whiteboard and markers
- a pack of colored pencils (at least two colors per student)
- optional: statements to read or project on the wall for the Open exercise
- optional: a large cake and several tubes of icing (one tube for every two or three students). You may want to write "Happy Birthlife!" in icing on the cake.
- optional: large-tip markers and a giant cake drawn on butcher paper

2. Session Intro

GOALS OF SESSION 3

As students experience this session, they will—
- gain a true understanding (as opposed to a cliché understanding) of the phrase *born again.*
- make a connection between their spiritual birth and God's eternal time clock.
- be invited to acknowledge their spiritual birth in a unique way.

PRAYER

OPEN: *WHO SAID IT?*
Group Contest: Guess who said these famous lines spoken at the dawn of something big.

3. Digging In: *Nic at Night*

Group Dig: Explore Jesus' words about spiritual birth.

4. Insight: *Deep Background*

Provide general background on the Pharisees, personal background on Nicodemus, and historic background on the phrase *born again*.

5. Digging Deeper: *Belief Benefits*

Group Dig: Discover that believing has its privileges.

6. Cross-Checking: *Do Over*

Personal Retreat: Breathe new life into the phrase *born again* by seeing what has to happen for us to enjoy the privileges of believing.

7. Taking It Inward: *A New Kind of Birthday*

Group Interaction: Help each other resist the urge to be like Nicodemus and instead, embrace Jesus' words about a second birthday.

8. Wrapping It Up: *It's Party Time!*

Group Interaction: Throw a "Happy Birthlife!" party!

1. Materials

For this session each student will need—
- the Session 3 Scripture sheet
- the student journal page for Session 3
- his or her own Bible, a pen, and a notebook

You'll also need—
- a whiteboard and markers
- a pack of colored pencils (at least two colors per student)
- optional: statements to read or project on the wall for the Open exercise
- optional: a large cake and several tubes of icing (one tube for every two or three students). You may want to write "Happy Birthlife!" in icing on the cake.
- optional: large-tip markers and a giant cake drawn on butcher paper

2. Session Intro

GOALS OF SESSION 3

As students experience this session, they will—
- gain a true understanding (as opposed to a cliché understanding) of the phrase *born again.*
- make a connection between their spiritual birth and God's eternal time clock.
- be invited to acknowledge their spiritual birth in a unique way.

PRAYER

OPEN: *WHO SAID IT?*
Group Interaction: Do a contest or group icebreaker on famous words spoken at the dawn of something big.

3. Digging In: *Nic at Night*

Group Dig: Explore Nic's questions and Jesus' words about spiritual birth.

4. Insight: *Deep Background*

Provide general background on the Pharisees, personal background on Nicodemus, and historic background on the phrase *born again*.

5. Digging Deeper: *Belief Benefits*

Group Dig: Discover that believing has its privileges.

6. Cross-Checking: *Do Over*

Personal Retreat: Breathe new life into the phrase *born again* by exploring other scripture passages on the subject.

7. Taking It Inward: *A New Kind of Birthday*

Group Interaction: Help each other resist the urge to be like Nicodemus and instead, embrace Jesus' words about a second birthday.

8. Wrapping It Up: *It's Party Time!*

Group Interaction: Throw a "Happy Birthlife!" party!

1. Materials

For this session each student will need—
- the Session 3 Scripture sheet
- the student journal page for Session 3
- his or her own Bible, a pen, and a notebook

You'll also need—
- a whiteboard and markers
- a pack of colored pencils (at least two colors per student)
- optional: statements to read or project on the wall for the Open exercise
- optional: materials for making birthday cards, such as felt-tip markers and card-stock paper

2. Session Intro

GOALS OF SESSION 3
As students experience this session, they will—
- gain a true understanding (as opposed to a cliché understanding) of the phrase *born again.*
- make a connection between their spiritual birth and God's eternal time clock.
- be invited to acknowledge their spiritual birth in a unique way.

PRAYER

OPEN: *WHO SAID IT?*
Group Interaction: Do a contest or group icebreaker on famous words spoken at the dawn of something big.

3. Digging In: *Nic at Night*

Group Dig: Explore Nic's questions and Jesus' words about spiritual birth.

4. Insight: *Deep Background*

Provide general background on the Pharisees, personal background on Nicodemus, and historic background on the phrase *born again*.

5. Digging Deeper: *Belief Benefits*

Group Dig: Discover that believing has its privileges.

6. Cross-Checking: *Do Over*

Personal Retreat: Breathe new life into the phrase *born again* by exploring other scripture passages on the subject.

7. Taking It Inward: *A New Kind of Birthday*

Group Interaction: Help each other resist the urge to be like Nicodemus and instead, embrace Jesus' words about a second birthday.

8. Wrapping It Up: *It's Party Time!*

Group Interaction: Throw a "Happy Birthlife!" party!

1. Materials

For this session each student will need—
- his or her own Bible
- optional: the student journal page for Session 3 (Using the student journal page is optional in the coffeehouse setting since table space will be limited.)

You'll also need—
- a pack of pencils with erasers
- optional: statements to read for the Open exercise
- optional: a food item from where you're meeting that can represent a birthday cake (enough for each student to have a bite)
- optional: a printed picture of a birthday cake with room to write names on the cake
- optional: a few spare Bibles for students who've forgotten theirs

2. Session Intro

Goals of Session 3

As students experience this session, they will—
- gain a true understanding (as opposed to a cliché understanding) of the phrase *born again.*
- make a connection between their spiritual birth and God's eternal time clock.
- be invited to acknowledge their spiritual birth in a unique way.

PRAYER

OPEN: *WHO SAID IT?*
Group Interaction: Ask students to guess who said these famous words spoken at the dawn of something big.

3. Digging In: *Nic at Night*

Group Dig: Explore Nic's questions and Jesus' words about spiritual birth.

4. Insight: *Deep Background*

Provide general background on the Pharisees, personal background on Nicodemus, and historic background on the phrase *born again*.

5. Digging Deeper: *Belief Benefits*

Group Dig: Discover that believing has its privileges.

6. Cross-Checking: *Do Over*

Group Dig: Explore a little more what Scripture says about new birth.

7. Taking It Inward: *A New Kind of Birthday*

Group Interaction: Help each other resist the urge to be like Nicodemus and instead, embrace Jesus' words about a second birthday.

8. Wrapping It Up: *It's Party Time!*

Group Interaction: Throw a "Happy Birthlife!" party! (In a coffeehouse sort of way.)

1. Materials (Optional)

- Sports Victory Clip: Search on a video-sharing Web site such as YouTube for a short video clip of a climactic sports victory. Use search terms such as *walk-off home run* or *buzzer-beaters*. You may also be able to get a clip from your students. Be sure the clip shows some fan pandemonium.
- Baby pictures of your students to project (Ask for these from parents ahead of time.)

2. Optional Opens

Movie Clip: Show a climactic sports ending such as a walk-off home run from a baseball game or a buzzer-beater shot from a basketball game.

Visual Illustration: photo presentation of student baby pictures

Quotations: a notable quotation on the concept of new birth and change

3. Digging In

Personal Story: Share about a new beginning or turning-point event when everything changed.
John 3:1-3, 16-21

4. Taking It Inward

God's Perspective: how God reacts when one of his children experiences rebirth

Our Perspective: What if we celebrated our spiritual births as God does?

5. Wrapping It Up

Challenge the students to examine whether or not we've been born again—and if we have, to celebrate it!

SESSION 4

Setting the Heart

How would you describe your worship experiences over the past month? Think about it for a minute...we'll wait!

As you picture your worship times in your mind's eye, are you picturing what it's like to be in God's presence—or has your worship fallen a bit short of that? Because we're flesh, in times of worship we have a natural tendency to be distracted by the things of the flesh—the size of the crowd, church duties, song tempos, what people are wearing—all kinds of things that have little to do with true worship! And here's another thought: If we're not careful, our worship can become nothing more than a flesh experience—full of warm moments, but completely lacking God's presence.

In John 4 we encounter a familiar scene: Jesus' interaction with the woman at the well. Although this scene isn't often associated with worship, we'll discover it has everything to do with the kind of worship our Father desires. Prepare your heart to study John 4 by meditating on the verses below—a word God gave his people at a time when the things of the world were greatly distracting them.

> "Woe to him who says to wood, 'Come to life!' Or to lifeless stone, 'Wake up!' Can it give guidance? It is covered with gold and silver; there is no breath in it. But the LORD is in his holy temple; let all the earth be silent before him." (Habakkuk 2:19-20)

Digging In

Testing the Waters

Read John 4:1-15 using your Scripture sheet.

As you read—

mark every mention of water (perhaps with a wave 〰). You'll notice two types of water in this passage, so you may want to use two colors to distinguish physical water (the water from the well) from spiritual water (the water Jesus offers).

Now let's make some observations on this famous scene.

List below everything you learn about the water Jesus offers.

How did the woman respond to Jesus' description of his water?

How did the woman's mindset differ from Jesus' mindset? What contrast(s) do you see?

Digging Deeper

This Just In

Using your Scripture sheet, read John 4:15-26. You'll notice that as the discussion unfolds between Jesus and the Samaritan woman, Jesus gradually reveals new information about himself. How does the woman's perspective of Jesus change as the conversation unfolds?

Now let's put the whole passage (John 4:1-26) together. Look back at the verses listed below, and mark every mention of Jesus with a cross ✝. Then record each new fact Jesus reveals about himself beside its verse reference.

4:9 _____

4:10 _____

4:14 _____

4:19 _____

4:25-26 _____

Pause to meditate on verses 20-24. List below everything Jesus taught the woman (and us!) about worship.

Jesus' Teachings on Worship

Take a second to put yourself in this woman's shoes. When she first encountered Jesus, she saw him as a common Jew. But by the end of this scene, Jesus had revealed himself to her as the Messiah! Throughout the exchange, Jesus taught the woman about two important spiritual concepts: his living water and true worship.

Did you notice as the woman listened to Jesus, she couldn't seem to break free from a *physical* mindset, though Jesus was talking about *spiritual* things? Describe what you see.

In what ways are you like this woman? What in your life tends to distract you from the spiritual things Jesus is trying to teach or give you?

What is God saying to you about his living water? Read John 4:13-14 again and journal below the thoughts of your heart.

How is the Father convicting you regarding true worship? Refer to John 4:23-24, and again, journal your thoughts.

Cross-Checking

The Perfect Metaphor

John 4 isn't the first time—or the last—that Scripture links the image of water with salvation. Read the passages below from your Bible. As you read, jot what you learn about salvation and/or spiritual water.

Isaiah 12:1-3

Isaiah 49:8-10

John 7:37-39

Revelation 21:5-6, 22:17

Taking It Inward

The Truth of Worship

Think about the parallels between Jesus' teachings on living water and on worship. Like Nicodemus in John 3, the Samaritan woman found it hard to see beyond the physical realm, whether Jesus was talking about water or worship. Caught up in the physical aspects of worship, she could only think about location. Focused on the body's physical need for water, she said, in essence, "Give it to me! Then I'll never have to drag my bucket to this well again!"

But Jesus persisted in revealing the true nature of worship and salvation, which happen in the spiritual realm. Let the questions below prompt you to respond to this truth—and let Jesus show you the true nature of worship and salvation.

Look again at John 4:23. What type of worshiper is God looking for?

When you worship, what does your mind typically dwell on?

The opposite of worshiping in spirit is worshiping in the physical realm. In what ways is it easy for us to worship in the physical realm?

How can our church traditions and rituals inhibit or enhance worshiping in spirit?

What ultimate truth did Jesus convey to the Samaritan woman in John 4:25-26, and how does that relate to "worshiping in truth"?

John uses the word *truth* (and quotes Jesus using it) more than any other Gospel writer. Look back over your study notes and Scripture sheets on John 1–3. List below at least five statements that express the truth of who Jesus is.

When you gather with others to worship, are you worshiping Jesus in truth? Are you worshiping him according to the true picture of him you've seen portrayed in the Gospels? Or, are you worshiping a picture of Jesus that's been handed to you through your heritage and tradition? How can you know the difference?

Look again at John 4:14 and 7:38 (see Cross-Checking). Do these verses describe you? What in your life needs to change so that you can have—as the New American Standard version puts it—"rivers of living water" flowing from your "innermost being"?

Wrapping It Up

Jesus-Style Worship

Select the appropriate Teach It guide for your session (full Teach It guides are on the CD-ROM accompanying this book). Then read through the guide so you're familiar with the flow of the session and confident with each exercise. Be sure to allow time for printing or photocopying student pages and pulling together any materials needed (see the Materials step in the Teach It guide).

Exercise Heads-Up: The Session 6 Teach It session for High School 1 calls for a video option (Digging Deeper Option 2: Video Recap) that will require some advance preparation, including recruiting a few students. You may want to look at that option now if you're using that guide.

Pray for yourself and your students between now and the group session. Pray that their hearts will be open to worshiping the Lord like they've never worshiped before: apart from the physical realm (music styles and tempos) and apart from the familiar (traditions that have been handed down), driven by the truth of who Jesus is and what he's done for them.

You may want to schedule a time when your group can experience worshiping in spirit and in truth. Let the content of John 4 frame your worship structure. Meet in a way that deliberately sets aside potential distractions and rituals.

WEB SUPPORT:
Remember to check out Web support for *See, Believe, Live* at www.inword.org. You'll find updated media suggestions (music, video clips), along with additional prep helps and even more application ideas. When at www.inword.org, look for the Digging Deeper series icon. You'll find password information in the Instructions at the front of this book.

Bonus Round

The Story Continues

John 4 covers more ground than we're dealing with in this session. You can use the following exercise to continue your encounter with Jesus and to get a grasp of the entire chapter before your group meets.

READ JOHN 4:27-42

Where did this event take place?

What did the Samaritan woman do after talking with Jesus?

What impact did she have on the people of her city?

READ JOHN 4:43-45

Where did this event take place?

How was Jesus received there?

READ JOHN 4:46-54

Where did this event take place?

To refresh your memory, write out John's purpose in writing this book (John 20:31).

How does this event relate to John's purpose in writing his Gospel?

John 4:1-26

1 The Pharisees heard that Jesus was gaining and baptizing more disciples than John,

2 although in fact it was not Jesus who baptized, but his disciples.

3 When the Lord learned of this, he left Judea and went back once more to Galilee.

4 Now he had to go through Samaria.

5 So he came to a town in Samaria called Sychar, near the plot of ground Jacob had given to his son Joseph.

6 Jacob's well was there, and Jesus, tired as he was from the journey, sat down by the well. It was about the sixth hour.

7 When a Samaritan woman came to draw water, Jesus said to her, "Will you give me a drink?"

8 (His disciples had gone into the town to buy food.)

9 The Samaritan woman said to him, "You are a Jew and I am a Samaritan woman. How can you ask me for a drink?" (For Jews do not associate with Samaritans.)

10 Jesus answered her, "If you knew the gift of God and who it is that asks you for a drink, you would have asked him and he would have given you living water."

11 "Sir," the woman said, "you have nothing to draw with and the well is deep. Where can you get this living water?

12 Are you greater than our father Jacob, who gave us the well and drank from it himself, as did also his sons and his flocks and herds?"

13 Jesus answered, "Everyone who drinks this water will be thirsty again,

14 but whoever drinks the water I give him will never thirst. Indeed, the water I give him will become in him a spring of water welling up to eternal life."

15 The woman said to him, "Sir, give me this water so that I won't get thirsty and have to keep coming here to draw water."

16 He told her, "Go, call your husband and come back."

17 "I have no husband," she replied. Jesus said to her, "You are right when you say you have no

husband.

18 The fact is, you have had five husbands, and the man you now have is not your husband. What you have just said is quite true."

19 "Sir," the woman said, "I can see that you are a prophet.

20 Our fathers worshiped on this mountain, but you Jews claim that the place where we must worship is in Jerusalem."

21 Jesus declared, "Believe me, woman, a time is coming when you will worship the Father neither on this mountain nor in Jerusalem.

22 You Samaritans worship what you do not know; we worship what we do know, for salvation is from the Jews.

23 Yet a time is coming and has now come when the true worshipers will worship the Father in spirit and truth, for they are the kind of worshipers the Father seeks.

24 God is spirit, and his worshipers must worship in spirit and in truth."

25 The woman said, "I know that Messiah" (called Christ) "is coming. When he comes, he will explain everything to us."

26 Then Jesus declared, "I who speak to you am he."

1. Materials

For this session each student will need—
- the Session 4 Scripture sheet
- the student journal page for Session 4
- his or her own Bible, a pen, and a notebook

You'll also need—
- a whiteboard and markers
- a pack of colored pencils (at least two colors per student)
- a large compass
- three or four small magnets per student (You can purchase packs of 20 round magnets in the craft section of Kmart or Wal-Mart or at a craft-supply store.)

2. Session Intro

GOALS OF SESSION 4
As students experience this session, they will—
- examine the details of a dialogue between Jesus and a Samaritan woman.
- discover the kind of worshiper for whom God is looking.
- be challenged to become that kind of worshiper.

PRAYER

OPEN: *DISTRACTIONS*
Introduce the idea of distractions with a compass and a magnet.

3. Digging In: *Testing the Waters*

Group Dig: Explore John 4:1-15 to discover what Jesus had to say about his water system.

4. Digging Deeper: *This Just In*

Personal Retreat: Investigate Jesus' specifics on worship.

5. Cross-Checking: *The Perfect Metaphor*

Personal Retreat: Look at one other time when Jesus spoke about living water.

6. Taking It Inward: *The Truth of Worship*

Group Interaction: Discuss how you can be someone God can easily find.

7. Wrapping It Up: *Jesus-Style Worship*

Group Interaction: Give each other ideas on how to remove distractions from worship.

OUTLINE **HIGH SCHOOL 1** SESSION 4

1. Materials

For this session each student will need—
* the Session 4 Scripture sheet
* the student journal page for Session 4
* his or her own Bible, a pen, and a notebook

You'll also need—
* a whiteboard and markers
* a pack of colored pencils (at least two colors per student)

2. Session Intro

GOALS OF SESSION 4

As students experience this session, they will—
* examine the details of a dialogue between Jesus and a Samaritan woman.
* discover the kind of worshiper for whom God is looking.
* be challenged to become that kind of worshiper.

PRAYER

OPEN: *DISTRACTIONS*
Group Interaction: Brainstorm things that distract us in life and worship.

3. Digging In: *Testing the Waters*

Group Dig: Explore John 4:1-15 to discover what Jesus had to say about his water system and how well the woman understood it.

4. Digging Deeper: *This Just In*

Personal Retreat: Investigate Jesus' specifics on worship.

5. Cross-Checking: *The Perfect Metaphor*

Group Experience: Create a PowerPoint or MediaShout presentation with other water verses.

6. Taking It Inward: *The Truth of Worship*

Group Interaction: Discuss the worship God is looking for in comparison to the worship we currently experience.

7. Wrapping It Up: *Jesus-Style Worship*

Challenge the group to make the necessary changes to be worshipers God can easily find.

1. Materials

For this session each student will need—
- the Session 4 Scripture sheet
- the student journal page for Session 4
- his or her own Bible, a pen, and a notebook

You'll also need—
- a whiteboard and markers
- a pack of colored pencils (at least two colors per student)

2. Session Intro

GOALS OF SESSION 4

As students experience this session, they will—
- examine the details of a dialogue between Jesus and a Samaritan woman.
- discover the kind of worshiper for whom God is looking.
- be challenged to become that kind of worshiper.

PRAYER

OPEN: *DISTRACTIONS*
Group Interaction: Brainstorm things that distract us in life and worship.

3. Digging In: *Testing the Waters*

Group Dig: Explore John 4:1-15 to discover what Jesus had to say about his water system and how well the woman understood it.

4. Digging Deeper: *This Just In*

Personal Retreat: Discover the escalating revelation of the woman's perspective of Jesus, and pinpoint Jesus' teaching on worship.

5. Cross-Checking: *The Perfect Metaphor*

Personal Retreat: Explore several great passages that use water as a metaphor for salvation.

6. Taking It Inward: *The Truth of Worship*

Group Interaction: Discuss how we can worship in spirit rather than in the physical realm.

7. Wrapping It Up: *Jesus-Style Worship*

Challenge the group to make the necessary changes to be worshipers God can easily find.

1. Materials

For this session each student will need—
- the Session 4 Scripture sheet
- the student journal page for Session 4
- his or her own Bible, a pen, and a notebook

You'll also need—
- a whiteboard and markers
- a pack of colored pencils (at least two colors per student)

2. Session Intro

GOALS OF SESSION 4

As students experience this session, they will—
- examine the details of a dialogue between Jesus and a Samaritan woman.
- discover the kind of worshiper for whom God is looking.
- be challenged to become that kind of worshiper.

PRAYER

OPEN: *DISTRACTIONS*

Group Interaction: Brainstorm things that distract us in life and worship.

3. Digging In: *Testing the Waters*

Group Dig: Explore John 4:1-15 to discover what Jesus had to say about his water system and how well the woman understood it.

4. Digging Deeper: *This Just In*

Group Dig: Let Jesus' teaching on worship help us adjust our worship mindset.

5. Cross-Checking: *The Perfect Metaphor*

Personal Retreat: Explore several great passages that use water as a metaphor for salvation.

6. Taking It Inward: *The Truth of Worship*

Group Interaction: Discuss how we can worship in spirit rather than in the physical realm.

7. Wrapping It Up: *Jesus-Style Worship*

Challenge the group to make the necessary changes to be worshipers God can easily find.

1. Materials

For this session each student will need—
- his or her own Bible
- optional: the student journal page for Session 4 (Using the student journal page is optional in the coffeehouse setting since table space will be limited.)

You'll also need—
- a pack of pencils with erasers
- optional: a few spare Bibles for students who've forgotten theirs

2. Session Intro

GOALS OF SESSION 4
As students experience this session, they will—
- examine the details of a dialogue between Jesus and a Samaritan woman.
- discover the kind of worshiper for whom God is looking.
- be challenged to become that kind of worshiper.

PRAYER

OPEN: *DISTRACTIONS*
Group Interaction: Brainstorm things that distract us in life and worship.

3. Digging In: *Testing the Waters*

Group Dig: Explore John 4:1-15 to discover what Jesus had to say about his water system and how well the woman understood it.

4. Digging Deeper: *This Just In*

Group Dig and Discussion: Follow the woman's view of Jesus, and pinpoint Jesus' teaching on worship.

5. Taking It Inward: *The Truth of Worship*

Group Interaction: Discuss how we can worship in spirit rather than in the physical realm.

6. Wrapping It Up: *Jesus-Style Worship*

Challenge students to make some changes in worship that go beyond their group worship settings on Sunday, spilling over into everyday life.

1. Materials (Optional)

- Movie Clip: *Star Wars: Episode V - The Empire Strikes Back*. Scene: when Darth Vader reveals that he is Luke's father (Chapter 46—counter cues, 1:49:17 to 1:52:43), or another movie that depicts a revelation that changes everything
- Magic Eye poster or image projection: You can grab the image of the week at www. magiceye.com, or you may have a poster or calendar you can use. Feel free to use another optical illusion such as the old lady/young lady picture, which you can easily find with a Web search.

2. Optional Opens

Movie Clip: *Star Wars: Episode V - The Empire Strikes Back*, or another movie that depicts a revelation that changes everything
Visual Illustration: Magic Eye image or other optical illusion
Quotations: notable quotations that illustrate how epiphanies and understanding can change our behavior

3. Digging In

Personal Story: Share an experience of learning something that at first was difficult.
John 4:26-30

4. Taking It Inward

Challenge students to show the world that they "get it" by their actions—how they worship and treat others.

5. Wrapping It Up

Have or plan a time to practice worshiping Jesus distraction-free.

SESSION 5

Setting the Heart

The message of the gospel is disruptive. It compels us to break with our past...change the direction of our lives...turn our priorities upside down. In short, a real encounter with Jesus will shake up our casual routines! In fact, if the message of the gospel hasn't shaken you up, you probably should consider whether you've truly encountered Jesus.

In the scenes we'll look at today, the message of the gospel came like a lightning bolt to the multitudes listening to Jesus. The people certainly didn't expect what Jesus taught, and it caught most of them off guard. It may catch you off guard as well. As you prepare your heart, ponder the verses below from Luke—Jesus' own thoughts on the disruptive power of his message.

> "I have come to bring fire on the earth, and how I wish it were already kindled! But I have a baptism to undergo, and how distressed I am until it is completed! Do you think I came to bring peace on earth? No, I tell you, but division. From now on there will be five in one family divided against each other, three against two and two against three. They will be divided, father against son and son against father, mother against daughter and daughter against mother, mother-in-law against daughter-in-law and daughter-in-law against mother-in-law." (Luke 12:49-53)

Digging In

What I Saw at the Miracle Meal

The heart of this session is the last half of John 6. But to get a running start, let's check out the first half.

Read John 6:1-29 using your Scripture sheet. As you read—

1. Use three colors and symbols to mark the various people in this passage: the crowd , Jesus' disciples [12], and Jesus [†].

2. Key in on words such as *saw* and *realized* and draw a pair of eyes [o o] or glasses [glasses] over what the crowd saw.

After you've finished, look back at the pairs of eyes you marked in John 6:1-29. In the space below, note what the crowd saw and how they reacted in each instance.

What They Saw	Their Reaction

After Jesus miraculously fed them, the crowd tracked Jesus down, and he gave them a challenge (John 6:25-29). In your opinion, what was the ultimate goal of Jesus' challenge?

Digging Deeper

Crowd-Pleaser?

Now to the heart of John 6. The next passage is lengthy but vital, since Jesus is teaching the crowd more about the challenge he gave earlier.

Read John 6:30-71 using your Scripture sheet. As you read—

1. Underline Jesus' claims about himself.

2. Use a different color to circle what Jesus said about those who "come to" or "believe in" him.

Before we move on, do you remember what the crowd was originally looking for? Reread John 6:14-15 and 28-31; then note below the crowd's mindset.

Now look back over what you underlined in John 6:30-71. In the space below, list what Jesus said about himself.

Jesus on Jesus

Next, list what you learn about those who "come to" or "believe in" Jesus.

Jesus on Those Who Come to Him

Look again at the verses listed below. In the margin of your Scripture sheet, draw an appropriate face 😄 😣 😏 next to each verse, representing the crowd's attitude toward Jesus' teaching.

John 6:34	**John 6:60**
John 6:41	**John 6:66**
John 6:52	**John 6:68-69**

Now take a few minutes to process what you've seen by responding to these questions:

As you look at what Jesus said about himself, what was he asking the crowd to believe?

What was he offering to those who believed?

How did the crowd react to his offer?

What's significant about the people who walked away? (Be specific; consult verse 66 if necessary.)

Recalling what the crowd was originally looking for, why was Jesus' teaching so difficult?

How did Jesus' 12 disciples respond? Why?

What difference do you see between the crowd's focus and the Twelve's focus?

The crowd's focus:

The Twelve's focus:

Cross-Checking

Interrupting the Regularly Scheduled Programming

Did you notice that those who rejected Jesus' teaching and withdrew from him were called "disciples"? A disciple of Jesus didn't have to be one of the Twelve. Many people followed Jesus throughout his ministry and were often called disciples (e.g., Joseph of Arimathea, John 19:38). Think about what it must take for a "disciple" to walk away from Jesus. John 6 makes it clear that there are no casual followers of Jesus Christ. If we fully embrace Jesus' message, it will by definition disrupt our comfortable lives.

The tragedy is, if we think we can get away with being "casual" followers of Jesus—and if his message hasn't disrupted our lives—we're in for a rude awakening. Read the passages below, making notes on what you see. Keep in mind what you've seen in John 6—and open your heart to the possibility of following Jesus as you've never followed before.

Matthew 7:13-14

Matthew 16:24-27

Luke 13:24-30

Wrapping It Up

Broad Versus Narrow

Select the appropriate Teach It guide for your session (full Teach It guides are on the CD-ROM accompanying this book). Then read through the guide so you're familiar with the flow of the session and confident with each exercise. Be sure to allow time for printing or photocopying student pages and pulling together any materials needed (see the Materials step in the Teach It guide). You'll notice that one option for closing the session is to take communion as a group. This may require some extra prep on your part.

A HEADS-UP ON TIME: If your group's actual study time is much less than an hour, you may want to summarize the first half of John 6 (Digging In) for your students, then begin with Digging Deeper. In this case, have the group begin reading at John 6:25 rather than John 6:30.

Before you close your book, take a few minutes to pray for your students' hearts. Jesus' message in John 6 can be a positive disruptive force in young people's lives—but not if their mental picture of Christ is clouded by traditions, wrong expectations, and distractions. (Remember the "disciples" who departed from Jesus after hearing his challenging, disruptive words?) Jesus is inviting your group members to experience a rich intimacy with him. Pray they will grasp his words as the truth that leads to eternal life.

John 6:1-71

1   Some time after this, Jesus crossed to the far shore of the Sea of Galilee (that is, the Sea of Tiberias),

2   and a great crowd of people followed him because they saw the miraculous signs he had performed on the sick.

3   Then Jesus went up on a mountainside and sat down with his disciples.

4   The Jewish Passover Feast was near.

5   When Jesus looked up and saw a great crowd coming toward him, he said to Philip, "Where shall we buy bread for these people to eat?"

6   He asked this only to test him, for he already had in mind what he was going to do.

7   Philip answered him, "Eight months' wages would not buy enough bread for each one to have a bite!"

8   Another of his disciples, Andrew, Simon Peter's brother, spoke up,

9   "Here is a boy with five small barley loaves and two small fish, but how far will they go among so many?"

10 Jesus said, "Have the people sit down." There was plenty of grass in that place, and the men sat down, about five thousand of them.

11 Jesus then took the loaves, gave thanks, and distributed to those who were seated as much as they wanted. He did the same with the fish.

12 When they had all had enough to eat, he said to his disciples, "Gather the pieces that are left over. Let nothing be wasted."

13 So they gathered them and filled twelve baskets with the pieces of the five barley loaves left over by those who had eaten.

14 After the people saw the miraculous sign that Jesus did, they began to say, "Surely this is the Prophet who is to come into the world."

15 Jesus, knowing that they intended to come and make him king by force, withdrew again to a mountain by himself.

16 When evening came, his disciples went down to the lake,

17 where they got into a boat and set off across the lake for Capernaum. By now it was dark, and Jesus had not yet joined them.

18 A strong wind was blowing and the waters grew rough.

19 When they had rowed three or three and a half miles, they saw Jesus approaching the boat, walking on the water; and they were terrified.

20 But he said to them, "It is I; don't be afraid."

21 Then they were willing to take him into the boat, and immediately the boat reached the shore where they were heading.

22 The next day the crowd that had stayed on the opposite shore of the lake realized that only one boat had been there, and that Jesus had not entered it with his disciples, but that they had gone away alone.

23 Then some boats from Tiberias landed near the place where the people had eaten the bread after the Lord had given thanks.

24 Once the crowd realized that neither Jesus nor his disciples were there, they got into the boats and went to Capernaum in search of Jesus.

25 When they found him on the other side of the lake, they asked him, "Rabbi, when did you get here?"

26 Jesus answered, "I tell you the truth, you are looking for me, not because you saw miraculous signs but because you ate the loaves and had your fill.

27 Do not work for food that spoils, but for food that endures to eternal life, which the Son of Man will give you. On him God the Father has placed his seal of approval."

28 Then they asked him, "What must we do to do the works God requires?"

29 Jesus answered, "The work of God is this: to believe in the one he has sent."

30 So they asked him, "What miraculous sign then will you give that we may see it and believe you? What will you do?

31 Our forefathers ate the manna in the desert; as it is written: 'He gave them bread from heaven to eat.'"

32 Jesus said to them, "I tell you the truth, it is not Moses who has given you the bread from heaven,

but it is my Father who gives you the true bread from heaven.

33 For the bread of God is he who comes down from heaven and gives life to the world."

34 "Sir," they said, "from now on give us this bread."

35 Then Jesus declared, "I am the bread of life. He who comes to me will never go hungry, and he who believes in me will never be thirsty.

36 But as I told you, you have seen me and still you do not believe.

37 All that the Father gives me will come to me, and whoever comes to me I will never drive away.

38 For I have come down from heaven not to do my will but to do the will of him who sent me.

39 And this is the will of him who sent me, that I shall lose none of all that he has given me, but raise them up at the last day.

40 For my Father's will is that everyone who looks to the Son and believes in him shall have eternal life, and I will raise him up at the last day."

41 At this the Jews began to grumble about him because he said, "I am the bread that came down from heaven."

42 They said, "Is this not Jesus, the son of Joseph, whose father and mother we know? How can he now say, 'I came down from heaven'?"

43 "Stop grumbling among yourselves," Jesus answered.

44 "No one can come to me unless the Father who sent me draws him, and I will raise him up at the last day.

45 It is written in the Prophets: 'They will all be taught by God.' Everyone who listens to the Father and learns from him comes to me.

46 No one has seen the Father except the one who is from God; only he has seen the Father.

47 I tell you the truth, he who believes has everlasting life.

48 I am the bread of life.

49 Your forefathers ate the manna in the desert, yet they died.

50 But here is the bread that comes down from heaven, which a man may eat and not die.

51 I am the living bread that came down from heaven. If anyone eats of this bread, he will live forever. This bread is my flesh, which I will give for the life of the world."

52 Then the Jews began to argue sharply among themselves, "How can this man give us his flesh to eat?"

53 Jesus said to them, "I tell you the truth, unless you eat the flesh of the Son of Man and drink his blood, you have no life in you.

54 Whoever eats my flesh and drinks my blood has eternal life, and I will raise him up at the last day.

55 For my flesh is real food and my blood is real drink.

56 Whoever eats my flesh and drinks my blood remains in me, and I in him.

57 Just as the living Father sent me and I live because of the Father, so the one who feeds on me will live because of me.

58 This is the bread that came down from heaven. Your forefathers ate manna and died, but he who feeds on this bread will live forever."

59 He said this while teaching in the synagogue in Capernaum.

60 On hearing it, many of his disciples said, "This is a hard teaching. Who can accept it?"

61 Aware that his disciples were grumbling about this, Jesus said to them, "Does this offend you?

62 What if you see the Son of Man ascend to where he was before!

63 The Spirit gives life; the flesh counts for nothing. The words I have spoken to you are spirit and they are life.

64 Yet there are some of you who do not believe." For Jesus had known from the beginning which of them did not believe and who would betray him.

65 He went on to say, "This is why I told you that no one can come to me unless the Father has enabled him."

66 From this time many of his disciples turned back and no longer followed him.

67 "You do not want to leave too, do you?" Jesus asked the Twelve.

68 Simon Peter answered him, "Lord, to whom shall we go? You have the words of eternal life.

69 We believe and know that you are the Holy One of God."

70 Then Jesus replied, "Have I not chosen you, the Twelve? Yet one of you is a devil!"

71 (He meant Judas, the son of Simon Iscariot, who, though one of the Twelve, was later to betray him.)

1. Materials
For this session each student will need—
> - the Session 5 Scripture sheet
> - the student journal page for Session 5
> - his or her own Bible, a pen, and a notebook

You'll also need—
> - a whiteboard and markers
> - a pack of colored pencils (at least three colors per student)
> - masking tape or duct tape
> - two picnic baskets or paper grocery bags, 10 small loaves of bread, four cans of tuna fish, two tablecloths, eight paper plates, eight sets of plastic utensils/silverware, and eight plastic cups/glasses (Check to see if the cans of tuna fish need a can opener.)
> - one 3-by-5-inch card for each student
> - optional: grape juice, bread, small cups, and a basket or plate for communion (See the Optional Close in Wrapping It Up.)

2. Session Intro

GOALS OF SESSION 5
As students experience this session, they will—
> - examine the expectations and commitments of those who followed Jesus after seeing his miraculous signs.
> - compare their level of commitment to both the crowd's casual commitment and the apostles' genuine commitment.
> - be challenged to imitate the apostles' commitment.

PRAYER

OPEN: *LOAVES AND FISHES PICNIC RELAY*
Introduce Jesus' food miracle with this fun food relay.

3. Digging In: *What I Saw at the Miracle Meal*
Group Dig: Explore John 6:1-15 to lay the backdrop for one of Jesus' strongest teachings.

4. Digging Deeper: *Crowd-Pleaser?*

Personal Retreat: Discover what Jesus does when the crowd is in the palm of his hand.

5. Taking It Inward: *Crowd Comparison*

Group Interaction: Allow students to evaluate whether they're following the crowd or following Jesus.

6. Cross-Checking: *Interrupting the Regularly Scheduled Programming*

Group Read: Use Matthew 7:13-14 to challenge students on whether their commitment to Jesus is disruptive to their lives.

7. Wrapping It Up: *Broad Versus Narrow*

Personal Commitment: Give students a chance to commit to the disruptive intimacy to which Jesus is calling us.
Optional: Experience the Lord's Supper together.

1. Materials

For this session each student will need—
- the Session 5 Scripture sheet
- the student journal page for Session 5
- his or her own Bible, a pen, and a notebook

You'll also need—
- a whiteboard and markers
- a pack of colored pencils (at least three colors per student)
- various images or a video clip showing what a synchronized crowd can do with cards
- optional: grape juice, bread, small cups, and a basket or plate for communion (See the Optional Close in Wrapping It Up.)

2. Session Intro

GOALS OF SESSION 5
As students experience this session, they will—
- examine the expectations and commitments of those who followed Jesus after seeing his miraculous signs.
- compare their level of commitment to both the crowd's casual commitment and the apostles' genuine commitment.
- be challenged to imitate the apostles' commitment.

PRAYER

OPEN: *MOB MENTALITY*
Show images or a video clip of what a synchronized crowd can do with cards.

3. Digging In: *What I Saw at the Miracle Meal*

Group Dig: Explore John 6:1-31 to lay the backdrop for one of Jesus' strongest teachings.

4. Digging Deeper: *Crowd-Pleaser?*

Personal Retreat: Discover what Jesus does when the crowd is in the palm of his hand.

5. Taking It Inward: *Crowd Comparison*

Group Interaction: Allow students to evaluate whether they're following the crowd or following Jesus.

6. Cross-Checking: *Interrupting the Regularly Scheduled Programming*

Group Read: Use Matthew 7:13-14 to challenge students on whether their commitment to Jesus is disruptive to their lives.

7. Wrapping It Up: *Broad Versus Narrow*

Personal Commitment: Give students a chance to commit to the disruptive intimacy to which Jesus is calling us.
Optional Close: Experience the Lord's Supper together.

1. Materials

For this session each student will need—
- the Session 5 Scripture sheet
- the student journal page for Session 5
- his or her own Bible, a pen, and a notebook

You'll also need—
- a whiteboard and markers
- a pack of colored pencils (at least three colors per student)
- various images or a video clip showing what a synchronized crowd can do with cards
- optional: juice, bread, small cups, and a basket or plate for communion (See the Optional Close in Wrapping It Up.)

2. Session Intro

GOALS OF SESSION 5

As students experience this session, they will—
- examine the expectations and commitments of those who followed Jesus after seeing his miraculous signs.
- compare their level of commitment to both the crowd's casual commitment and the apostles' genuine commitment.
- be challenged to imitate the apostles' commitment.

PRAYER

OPEN: *MOB MENTALITY*

Show images or a video clip of what a synchronized crowd can do with cards.

3. Digging In: *What I Saw at the Miracle Meal*

Group Dig: Explore John 6:1-15 to lay the backdrop for one of Jesus' strongest teachings.

4. Digging Deeper: *Crowd-Pleaser?*

Personal Retreat: Discover in John 6:30-71 what Jesus does when the crowd is in the palm of his hand.

5. Taking It Inward: *Crowd Comparison*

Group Interaction: Allow students to evaluate whether they're following the crowd or following Jesus.

6. Cross-Checking: *Interrupting the Regularly Scheduled Programming*

Group Read: Use Matthew 7:13-14, Matthew 16:24-27, and Luke 13:24-30 to challenge students on whether their commitment to Jesus is disruptive to their lives.

7. Wrapping It Up: *Broad Versus Narrow*

Personal Commitment: Give students a chance to commit to the disruptive intimacy to which Jesus is calling us.
Optional Close: Experience the Lord's Supper together.

1. Materials

For this session each student will need—
- the Session 5 Scripture sheet
- the student journal page for Session 5
- his or her own Bible, a pen, and a notebook

You'll also need—
- a whiteboard and markers
- a pack of colored pencils (at least three colors per student)
- various images or a video clip showing what a synchronized crowd can do with cards
- optional: juice, bread, small cups, and a basket or plate for communion (See the Optional Close in Wrapping It Up.)

2. Session Intro

GOALS OF SESSION 5

As students experience this session, they will—
- examine the expectations and commitments of those who followed Jesus after seeing his miraculous signs.
- compare their level of commitment to both the crowd's casual commitment and the apostles' genuine commitment.
- be challenged to imitate the apostles' commitment.

PRAYER

OPEN: *MOB MENTALITY*

Show images or a video clip of what a synchronized crowd can do with cards.

3. Digging In: *What I Saw at the Miracle Meal*

Group Dig: Explore John 6:1-15 to lay the backdrop for one of Jesus' strongest teachings.

4. Digging Deeper: *Crowd-Pleaser?*

Personal Retreat: Discover in John 6:30-71 what Jesus does when the crowd is in the palm of his hand.

5. Taking It Inward: *Crowd Comparison*

Group Interaction: Allow students to evaluate whether they're following Jesus with "crowd mentality" or "The Twelve mentality."

6. Cross-Checking: *Interrupting the Regularly Scheduled Programming*

Group Read: Use Matthew 7:13-14, Matthew 16:24-27, and Luke 13:24-30 to challenge students on whether their commitment to Jesus is disruptive to their lives.

7. Wrapping It Up: *Broad Versus Narrow*

Personal Commitment: Give students a chance to commit to the disruptive intimacy to which Jesus is calling us.
Optional Close: Experience the Lord's Supper together.

1. Materials

For this session each student will need—
- his or her own Bible
- optional: the student journal page for Session 5 (Using the student journal page is optional in the coffeehouse setting since table space will be limited.)

You'll also need—
- optional: laptop with a wireless Internet connection to display various images or a video clip showing what a synchronized crowd can do with cards
- a pack of pencils with erasers
- optional: a few spare Bibles for students who've forgotten theirs

2. Session Intro

GOALS OF SESSION 5

As students experience this session, they will—
- examine the expectations and commitments of those who followed Jesus after seeing his miraculous signs.
- compare their level of commitment to both the crowd's casual commitment and the apostles' genuine commitment.
- be challenged to imitate the apostles' commitment.

PRAYER

OPEN: *MOB MENTALITY*
Video Clip: Show a clip of what a synchronized crowd can do with cards.

3. Digging In: *What I Saw at the Miracle Meal*

Group Dig: Explore John 6:1-15 to lay the backdrop for one of Jesus' strongest teachings.

4. Digging Deeper: *Crowd-Pleaser?*

Group Dig: Discover in John 6:30-56 what Jesus does when the crowd is in the palm of his hand.

5. Taking It Inward: *Crowd Comparison*

Group Interaction: Allow students to evaluate whether they're following Jesus with "crowd mentality" or "the Twelve mentality."

6. Cross-Checking: *Interrupting the Regularly Scheduled Programming*

Group Read: Use Matthew 7:13-14 to challenge students on whether their commitment to Jesus is disruptive to their lives.

7. Wrapping It Up: *Broad Versus Narrow*

Personal Commitment: Give students a chance to commit to the disruptive intimacy to which Jesus is calling us.
Optional: Schedule a time to experience the Lord's Supper together.

1. Materials (Optional)

- Movie/Video Clip: Show three to four minutes of a movie scene, or play a music video along the lines of "When the going gets tough, the tough get going" (a pep talk from a coach, a motivational talk from a military leader, etc.). You may be able to find a video montage of movie fight scenes called "Heroes in Training" at http://youtube.com/watch?v=Hpun38yBOOM.
- Leader List: Before the talk, list on poster board the names of famous people from history, e.g., Gandhi, Isaac Newton, Mother Teresa, Napoleon Bonaparte, the Wright Brothers, George Washington, Dr. Martin Luther King, Jr., and Jesus. Google a phrase like "100 most influential people" for more ideas.
- Quotations: Collect leadership statements from famous people to share with the students.

2. Optional Opens

Movie/Video Clip: movie scene or music video illustrating, "When the going gets tough, the tough get going"
Visual Illustration: how famous people stood up against the political, social, religious, or popular thinking of their day
Quotations: leadership statements from famous people

3. Digging In

Personal Story: Share a story about someone who made a decision to take a difficult road when he or she could have taken the easy way out.
John 6:53-69
Personal Illustration: Choosing Jesus often means you can't take the easy path.

4. Taking It Inward

God's Perspective: God calls us to choose his way because he knows what's best.
Our Perspective: Given the choice, we'll usually choose the way of least resistance instead of God's way.

5. Wrapping It Up

Matthew 7:13-14
Challenge: Invite students to choose the narrow way.

SESSION 6

Setting the Heart

It's probably no accident that the incidents of Jesus giving sight to the blind are recorded more than any other miracle in the Gospels. God is light. The world is dark. What better illustration is there of what God wants to do with the world than to have his Son bring light into impossibly dark situations?

Zechariah, the father of John the Baptist, prophesied about the light-giving work of Jesus while speaking to his newborn son. As you prepare your heart to experience one of Jesus' sight-giving miracles in John 9, read Zechariah's words below. Let God speak to you about what he wants to accomplish in your life.

> "And you, my child, will be called a prophet of the Most High; for you will go on before the Lord to prepare the way for him, to give his people the knowledge of salvation through the forgiveness of their sins, because of the tender mercy of our God, by which the rising sun will come to us from heaven to shine on those living in darkness and in the shadow of death, to guide our feet into the path of peace." (Luke 1:76-79)

Digging In

Here's Mud in Your Eye

Read John 9:1-7 using your Scripture sheet. As you read, do the following:

1. Mark a cross ✝ over every mention of Jesus.

2. Draw a pair of glasses 🕶 over every mention of the blind man.

3. Mark an "ichthus" ∝ over all mentions of the disciples.

Looking back at the Scripture you marked, why was the man born blind?

What are some possible meanings of the phrase *that the work of God might be displayed in his life*?

Digging Deeper

The Man Formerly Known as Blind

Jesus' healing of the blind man set off an amazing chain of events. One of the best ways to experience and understand events in Scripture is to ask the questions, *Who? What? When? Where?* and *Why?* as you read. For now, let's focus on the "who."

Read John 9:8-41 from your Scripture sheet.

> 1. Mark every reference to the blind man (who's now no longer blind).
>
> 2. Mark every mention of Jesus.
>
> 3. Mark every mention of other people, such as the crowd, the disciples, and the Jewish leaders. You could mark the crowd with some faces 😄 😄 😄, the disciples with an "ichthus" ⟨✕ , and the Jewish leaders with the Star of David ✡. Remember to mark pronouns such as *they* or *him*.

After you've read the chapter, it will help you to see it as a group of related scenes. Take a moment to look over what you marked; see if your markings help you divide the passage into scenes. It may help you to ask the questions, *What? When? and Where?* Then indicate the scene changes by drawing lines to separate them in the margin of your Scripture sheet. Now make a simple outline of the passage in the space below.

After the blind man was healed, he didn't get much time to celebrate. In fact, how did things get worse for him before they got better?

Jesus said the man was born blind so that the work of God might be displayed in his life—or *in him*. What did his blindness ultimately bring about?

Does this give you a clue as to what Jesus meant by the "work of God"?

Cross-Checking

Write If You Find Work

Perhaps you've noticed by now: The man wasn't born blind so that he could be an object lesson to the disciples and the crowd. *He* received the full benefit of the work of God—*he* was healed, *he* worshiped Jesus—and he *believed* in Jesus as the Son of God.

Just like the blind man, we're all able to be recipients of the work of God! Read the passages below from your Bible. Write what you learn about the work of God—what it is and what it's to accomplish.

John 5:35-40

John 6:28-29

Ephesians 2:1-10

Taking It Inward

Spiritual Blind Spots

Now that you've studied these cross-references, take another crack at explaining what Jesus meant by, "that the work of God might be displayed in his life."

In what ways are you experiencing spiritual "blindness" right now? As believers we don't typically think of ourselves as "spiritually blind." But are there temptations, struggles, or personal losses that are blinding you in some way?

How might God use this blindness to reveal his work in your life?

Who was the first person to seek out the blind man after the Pharisees cast him out of the synagogue? (See John 9:35.) What does this say to you?

Cross-Checking

The Cure for Darkness: Light

Whatever your area of blindness, Jesus will seek you out. Let him seek you, find you, and heal you—that the work of God might be revealed in your life. The passages below teach us how God's light can heal our blindness and darkness. Use the space beneath each verse reference to write a prayer—perhaps a confession, a request, or a prayer of thanksgiving.

2 Corinthians 4:5-18
(It's a big chunk, but there's no good place to stop! Just savor this incredible passage in light of John 9.)

Ephesians 5:8-14

1 Thessalonians 5:5-8

Insight

Just in Case

John 9 concludes with several statements from Jesus to the Pharisees that your group may find confusing. You won't cover these verses in the group session, but your students may bring them up. To prepare yourself for their questions, read John 9:39-41 carefully. Being as detailed as possible, list below what Jesus said about his judgment. Then read the following verses and do the same.

John 3:14-21

John 5:22-27

John 12:44-50

Now take a moment to summarize what you've learned about Jesus' judgment. Allow God's Spirit to give you understanding of his Word, and write your own commentary in the space below—in other words, how your understanding could help the next person who comes along to read this passage.

Please don't read this paragraph until you've recorded your thoughts above. As the verses you've studied show, Jesus himself wasn't a judge during his first coming to earth, but his presence brought judgment. If you're in darkness and realize that you need the light, you accept (believe) the light and see!

However, if you're in darkness but don't think you're in darkness, when you see the light, you reject the light and remain in darkness. This is what the Pharisees did in John 9. Thus, judgment is automatically rendered; people with this mindset are destined to continue in darkness.

Wrapping It Up

As you conclude this Prep It, pray that your group members will see their areas of blindness and have the courage to ask for Jesus' healing. Select the appropriate Teach It guide for your session (full Teach It guides are on the CD-ROM accompanying this book). Then read through the guide so you're familiar with the flow of the session and confident with each exercise. Be sure to allow time for printing or photocopying student pages and pulling together any materials needed (see the Materials step in the Teach It guide).

Before you close your book, take a moment to pray for your students—that their hearts will be open to the work God wants to do in their lives.

WEB SUPPORT:
Remember to check out Web support for *See, Believe, Live* at www.inword.org. You'll find updated media suggestions (music, video clips), along with additional prep helps and even more application ideas. When at www.inword.org, look for the Digging Deeper series icon. You'll find password information in the Instructions at the front of this book.

John 9:1-41

1   As he went along, he saw a man blind from birth.

2   His disciples asked him, "Rabbi, who sinned, this man or his parents, that he was born blind?"

3   "Neither this man nor his parents sinned," said Jesus, "but this happened so that the work of God might be displayed in his life.

4   As long as it is day, we must do the work of him who sent me. Night is coming, when no one can work.

5   While I am in the world, I am the light of the world."

6   Having said this, he spit on the ground, made some mud with the saliva, and put it on the man's eyes.

7   "Go," he told him, "wash in the Pool of Siloam" (this word means Sent). So the man went and washed, and came home seeing.

8   His neighbors and those who had formerly seen him begging asked, "Isn't this the same man who used to sit and beg?"

9   Some claimed that he was. Others said, "No, he only looks like him." But he himself insisted, "I am the man."

10   "How then were your eyes opened?" they demanded.

11   He replied, "The man they call Jesus made some mud and put it on my eyes. He told me to go to Siloam and wash. So I went and washed, and then I could see."

12   "Where is this man?" they asked him. "I don't know," he said.

13   They brought to the Pharisees the man who had been blind.

14   Now the day on which Jesus had made the mud and opened the man's eyes was a Sabbath.

15   Therefore the Pharisees also asked him how he had received his sight. "He put mud on my eyes," the man replied, "and I washed, and now I see."

16   Some of the Pharisees said, "This man is not from God, for he does not keep the Sabbath." But others asked, "How can a sinner do such miraculous signs?" So they were divided.

17 Finally they turned again to the blind man, "What have you to say about him? It was your eyes he opened." The man replied, "He is a prophet."

18 The Jews still did not believe that he had been blind and had received his sight until they sent for the man's parents.

19 "Is this your son?" they asked. "Is this the one you say was born blind? How is it that now he can see?"

20 "We know he is our son," the parents answered, "and we know he was born blind.

21 But how he can see now, or who opened his eyes, we don't know. Ask him. He is of age; he will speak for himself."

22 His parents said this because they were afraid of the Jews, for already the Jews had decided that anyone who acknowledged that Jesus was the Christ would be put out of the synagogue.

23 That was why his parents said, "He is of age; ask him."

24 A second time they summoned the man who had been blind. "Give glory to God," they said. "We know this man is a sinner."

25 He replied, "Whether he is a sinner or not, I don't know. One thing I do know. I was blind but now I see!"

26 Then they asked him, "What did he do to you? How did he open your eyes?"

27 He answered, "I have told you already and you did not listen. Why do you want to hear it again? Do you want to become his disciples, too?"

28 Then they hurled insults at him and said, "You are this fellow's disciple! We are disciples of Moses!

29 We know that God spoke to Moses, but as for this fellow, we don't even know where he comes from."

30 The man answered, "Now that is remarkable! You don't know where he comes from, yet he opened my eyes.

31 We know that God does not listen to sinners. He listens to the godly man who does his will.

32 Nobody has ever heard of opening the eyes of a man born blind.

33 If this man were not from God, he could do nothing."

34 To this they replied, "You were steeped in sin at birth; how dare you lecture us!" And they threw him out.

35 Jesus heard that they had thrown him out, and when he found him, he said, "Do you believe in the Son of Man?"

36 "Who is he, sir?" the man asked. "Tell me so that I may believe in him."

37 Jesus said, "You have now seen him; in fact, he is the one speaking with you."

38 Then the man said, "Lord, I believe," and he worshiped him.

39 Jesus said, "For judgment I have come into this world, so that the blind will see and those who see will become blind."

40 Some Pharisees who were with him heard him say this and asked, "What? Are we blind too?"

41 Jesus said, "If you were blind, you would not be guilty of sin; but now that you claim you can see, your guilt remains."

1. Materials

For this session each student will need—
- the Session 6 Scripture sheet
- the student journal page for Session 6
- his or her own Bible, a pen, and a notebook

You'll also need—
- a whiteboard and markers
- a pack of colored pencils (at least three colors per student)
- one 3-by-5-inch card for each student with "blind spot" items drawn on them (see open)
- optional: a few yardsticks
- marshmallows
- one pair of cheap plastic sunglasses with colored frames (so that marking on them in black will show up) for each student
- Black Sharpie markers
- optional: bucket (or bowl) of water labeled "Siloam"

2. Session Intro

GOALS OF SESSION 6

As students experience this session, they will—
- see what can happen when the work of God is displayed in a person.
- examine their personal "blind spots."
- be challenged to let the work of God be revealed in them by allowing Jesus to heal their spiritual "blind spots."

PRAYER

OPEN: *BLIND SPOTS*

Use the famous "blind spot" exercise to introduce students to the subject of healing our blind spots.

3. Digging In: *Here's Mud in Your Eye*

Group Dig: Explore John 9:1-7 to uncover events that set the stage for a mighty work of God.

4. Digging Deeper: *The Man Formerly Known as Blind*

Reading Drama: Use this impromptu drama to give students an overview of the action in John 9.

5. Cross-Checking: *Write If You Find Work*

Group Read: Let John 6:28-29 shed light on the meaning of "the work of God."

6. Taking It Inward: *Shades of Blindness*

Group Interaction: Use cheap sunglasses to help students process their personal spiritual blind spots.

7. Cross-Checking: *The Cure for Darkness: Light*

Personal Retreat: Students will read a passage that explains how Jesus still heals our blindness.

8. Wrapping It Up: *The Bucket of Siloam*

Group Exercise: Create a "pool of Siloam" to help students experience healing from Jesus.

1. Materials

For this session each student will need—
- the Session 6 Scripture sheet
- the student journal page for Session 6
- his or her own Bible, a pen, and a notebook

You'll also need—
- a whiteboard and markers
- a pack of colored pencils (at least three colors per student)
- two slips of paper per student
- optional: video-clip recap of John 9 from a video-sharing Web site such as YouTube or Google Video. You should find several options by simply searching *John 9 blind man*.
- optional: bucket (or bowl) of water labeled "Siloam"

2. Session Intro

GOALS OF SESSION 6

As students experience this session, they will—
- see what can happen when the work of God is displayed in a person.
- examine their personal "blind spots."
- be challenged to let the work of God be revealed in them by allowing Jesus to heal their spiritual "blind spots."

PRAYER

OPEN: *MIRACLE POLL*
Open by polling your students on the different miracles Jesus performed.

3. Digging In: *Here's Mud in Your Eye*

Group Dig: Explore John 9:1-7 to uncover events that set the stage for a mighty work of God.

4. Digging Deeper: *The Man Formerly Known as Blind*

Option 1: Reading Drama. Use this impromptu drama to give students an overview of the action in John 9.
Option 2: Video Experience. Use video clips or a homemade video with your students to cover some of the action in John 9.

5. Cross-Checking: *Write If You Find Work*

Group Read: Let John 6:28-29 shed light on the meaning of "the work of God."

6. Taking It Inward: *Shades of Blindness*

Group Interaction: Use this exercise to help students process their personal spiritual blind spots.

7. Cross-Checking: *The Cure for Darkness: Light*

Personal Retreat: Students will read a passage that explains how Jesus still heals our blindness.

8. Wrapping It Up: *The Bucket of Siloam*

Group Exercise: Create a "pool of Siloam" to help students experience healing from Jesus.

1. Materials

For this session each student will need—
- the Session 6 Scripture sheet
- the student journal page for Session 6
- his or her own Bible, a pen, and a notebook

You'll also need—
- a whiteboard and markers
- a pack of colored pencils (at least three colors per student)
- two slips of paper per student
- optional: video-clip recap of John 9 from a video-sharing Web site such as YouTube or Google Video. You should find several options by simply searching *John 9 blind man.*
- optional: bucket (or bowl) of water labeled "Siloam"

2. Session Intro

GOALS OF SESSION 6

As students experience this session, they will—
- see what can happen when the work of God is displayed in a person.
- examine their personal "blind spots."
- be challenged to let the work of God be revealed in them by allowing Jesus to heal their spiritual "blind spots."

PRAYER

OPEN: *MIRACLE POLL*

Open by polling your students on the different miracles Jesus performed.

3. Digging In: *Here's Mud in Your Eye*

Group Dig: Explore John 9:1-7 to uncover events that set the stage for a mighty work of God.

4. Digging Deeper: *The Man Formerly Known as Blind*

Option 1: Group Dig. Explore John 9:8-41 to give students an overview of the drama in this chapter.

Option 2: Video Experience. Use video clips from YouTube to cover some of the action in John 9.

5. Cross-Checking: *Write If You Find Work*

Group Read: Let several passages shed light on the meaning of "the work of God."

6. Taking It Inward: *Shades of Blindness*

Group Interaction: Use this exercise to help students process their personal spiritual blind spots.

7. Cross-Checking: *The Cure for Darkness: Light*

Personal Retreat: Students will read passages that explain how Jesus still heals our blindness.

8. Wrapping It Up: *The Bucket of Siloam*

Group Exercise: Create a "pool of Siloam" to help students experience healing from Jesus.

1. Materials

For this session each student will need—
- the Session 6 Scripture sheet
- the student journal page for Session 6
- his or her own Bible, a pen, and a notebook

You'll also need—
- optional: a video from YouTube or Google Video that depicts the scene in John 9
- a whiteboard and markers
- a pack of colored pencils (at least three colors per student)

2. Session Intro

GOALS OF SESSION 6
As students experience this session, they will—
- see what can happen when the work of God is displayed in a person.
- examine their personal "blind spots."
- be challenged to let the work of God be revealed in them by allowing Jesus to heal their spiritual "blind spots."

PRAYER

OPEN: *MIRACLE POLL*
Open by polling your students on the different miracles Jesus performed.

3. Digging In: *Here's Mud in Your Eye*

Group Dig: Explore John 9:1-7 to uncover events that set the stage for a mighty work of God.

4. Digging Deeper: *The Man Formerly Known as Blind*

Option 1: Group Dig. Explore John 9:8-41 to give students an overview of the drama in this chapter.
Option 2: Video Experience. Use video clips from YouTube to cover some of the action in John 9.

5. Cross-Checking: *Write If You Find Work*

Group Read: Let several passages shed light on the meaning of "the work of God."

6. Taking It Inward: *Spiritual Blind Spot*

Group Interaction: Use this exercise to help students process their personal spiritual blind spots.

7. Cross-Checking: *The Cure for Darkness: Light*

Personal Retreat: Students will read passages that explain how Jesus still heals our blindness.

8. Wrapping It Up: *The Bucket of Siloam*

Group Interaction: Invite students to share their spiritual blind spots with each other.

1. Materials

For this session each student will need—
- his or her own Bible
- optional: the student journal page for Session 6 (Using the student journal page is optional in the coffeehouse setting since table space will be limited.)

You'll also need—
- one napkin per student
- optional: laptop with wireless Internet connection for showing a video that depicts the scene in John 9
- optional: a cup (or bowl) of water labeled "Siloam"
- a pack of pencils with erasers
- optional: a few spare Bibles for students who've forgotten theirs

2. Session Intro

GOALS OF SESSION 6

As students experience this session, they will—
- see what can happen when the work of God is displayed in a person.
- examine their personal "blind spots."
- be challenged to let the work of God be revealed in them by allowing Jesus to heal their spiritual "blind spots."

PRAYER

OPEN: *MIRACLE POLL*
Open by polling your students on the different miracles Jesus performed.

3. Digging In: *Here's Mud in Your Eye*

Group Dig: Explore John 9:1-7 to uncover events that set the stage for a mighty work of God.

4. Digging Deeper: *The Man Formerly Known as Blind*

Option 1: Video Experience. Use video clips from YouTube to cover some of the action in John 9.

Option 2: "Bullet Me" Experience. Use these bullet points to bring your students up to speed on the drama in John 9:8-38.

5. Cross-Checking: *Write If You Find Work*

Group Read: Let John 6:28-29 shed light on the meaning of "the work of God."

6. Taking It Inward: *Spiritual Blind Spots*

Group Exercise: Use this exercise to help students process their personal spiritual blind spots.

7. Cross-Checking: *The Cure for Darkness: Light*

Group Read: Let 2 Corinthians 4:5-18 explain how Jesus still heals our blindness.

8. Wrapping It Up: *The Bucket of Siloam*

Group Exercise: Create a "pool of Siloam" to help students experience healing from Jesus.

1. Materials (Optional)

- A candle, match or lighter, lamp, flashlights and/or keychain lights, and a few students to act as "ushers"
- Pre-Session Video: If your group is too big or your meeting room is too well-lit to make it dark enough, make a video of the visual illustration below. Show the video instead of doing the exercise in the group setting.

2. Optional Opens

Visual Illustration: Gradually change the room lighting from dark to well-lit.
Video: Conduct the illustration before your session and interview students about what happened when the room went from dark to well-lit.
Story: Share about a long or untimely power outage.

3. Digging In

John 9:24-25
Personal Story: Share your personal testimony couched in terms of darkness/blindness versus light/sight, emphasizing that we all start out blind.
1 Thessalonians 5:5-8

4. Taking It Inward

Jesus sought out the man formerly known as blind and asked him a question that would usher in the works of God: "Do you believe?"

5. Wrapping It Up

Challenge students to see Jesus in our dark situations and experience him as the light of the world.

SESSION 7

Setting the Heart

Saying yes to any ministry endeavor can be a risky proposition. Anything you say in the work of ministry *can* and *will* be used against you if it's not in accordance with God's Word! Anything that's not pure gospel—pure *truth*—has the potential to rob God's people of the abundant life Jesus promised. Take a moment to empty your heart before the Lord. Set aside the busyness of ministry, along with anything else that may be consuming your thoughts right now. Then fill your mind with these wise words from Peter.

> Whoever speaks, is to do so as one who is speaking the utterances of God; whoever serves is to do so as one who is serving by the strength which God supplies; so that in all things God may be glorified through Jesus Christ, to whom belongs the glory and dominion forever and ever. Amen. (1 Peter 4:11, NAS)

Digging In

What's a Metaphor? (To Keep the Sheep In)

John 10 continues a dialogue that began in John 9. So to get a running start on John 10, read John 9:35-41 from your Bible or Session 6 Scripture sheet. Be sure to notice Jesus' audience.

Now read John 10:1-18 using your Session 7 Scripture sheet.

1. Mark every mention of Jesus (including those in Jesus' illustration) with a cross .

2. Mark every mention of the various people or animals in Jesus' illustration (such as the thief, the sheep, etc.) in different colors so you're able to identify them easily.

If you paid attention in high school English, you know that a *metaphor* is a figurative expression in which two things are compared *without* the use of comparison words, such as *like, as,* or *such as*. (For example, Jesus uses two metaphors in John 15:5: "I am the vine; you are the branches.") List below each of the metaphors Jesus uses in John 10:1-18.

Now list below everything you learn about thieves and robbers. (Be sure to start at verse 1.)

Who might the thieves and robbers represent? Before answering this question, you may need to dispense with any preconceived notions you have about the thief. When part of this passage is quoted alone—as it often is—it appears that Jesus is referring to Satan. Indeed, Satan is a thief; but considering the info you've gathered so far, could anyone else be considered "thieves and robbers"? Write down the possibilities that come to mind.

Cross-Checking

More on Sheep and Shepherds

In the space below, record the group Jesus was addressing in this passage.

Keep in mind that these folks were the spiritual leaders of their day—the ones who should have been most adept at understanding Jesus' point. Let's look at a few Old Testament prophecies with which the Pharisees would have been familiar. These passages can give us insight into Jesus' illustration.

Jeremiah 23:1-10
What were the shepherds (spiritual leaders in the verse) doing or not doing? Be as detailed as possible.

What was God going to do in response to the actions of these shepherds?

Where do you see Jesus in this passage? What does God say about him?

Ezekiel 34:1-16

In this passage, what were the shepherds doing or not doing? (Again, be specific.)

What was God going to do in response to the shepherds' actions?

Taking It Inward

Perfect Gate, Perfect Shepherd

Now let's examine what God is saying to us as spiritual leaders. What words would you use to describe the spiritual leaders of Israel in Jeremiah and Ezekiel's day?

Did these verses give you any insight into who the thief might be in John 10:10?

Taking into account what Jesus said about thieves and robbers (they came before Jesus, they don't enter through the gate, etc.)—and paralleling his words with those of Jeremiah and Ezekiel— does it seem to you that the thieves in John 10 could be the corrupt spiritual leaders of God's flock?

Think for a moment about what can get today's spiritual leaders off track. List your ideas below.

Thankfully, the good shepherd, the Lord Our Righteousness, has come to lead us. Look back at the verses in which Jesus describes himself as the shepherd and the gate in John 10. List below everything you learn about Jesus through these metaphors.

Jesus as the Gate	Jesus as the Shepherd

In John 10:7-18, who might the hired hand and the wolf represent?

How does Jesus' protection of and care for the sheep compare with that of the hired hand? (Be sure to note the full extent of Jesus' protection.)

The "hired hands" of today could be pastors and ministers, including those who work or volunteer with youth. So let's take a moment to see how Jesus' metaphor applies to us personally.

In your ministry, what are you doing to help your "flock" be truly led by the good shepherd, who laid down his life for them?

Are there any ways you're directing more attention to the hired hand (you!) rather than the good shepherd? What needs to change so that all the attention goes to the good shepherd?

How does your "flock" compare to the sheep in Ezekiel 34? Are any of them weak? Sickly? Have any gone astray? Have you treated any of them harshly? What is your responsibility?

Think about the warnings and conditions of spiritual leadership given in Jeremiah and Ezekiel. Do you get your ministry "agenda" from the good shepherd and his Word? Or do others' opinions and methods (e.g., books, training seminars, schooling, etc.) mostly drive your ministry?

What changes can be made in your approach to ministry to ensure that students are being cared for more by the good shepherd and less by "hired hands"? (If you're short on ideas, go back to 1 Peter 4:11, the Setting the Heart passage for this Prep It.)

Digging Deeper

Be a Sheep!

So far we've looked at the responsibilities of shepherds in John 10 and related passages. Now let's focus on the sheep. Read John 10:19-30 using your Scripture sheet. Use the same color or symbol you used earlier to mark every mention of sheep.

Now list everything you learn about Jesus' sheep.

Jesus' Sheep

Insight

Sheepy Facts

Jesus, the master teacher, often used simple, everyday objects and actions to explain spiritual truth. In this instance, he borrows an illustration from the shepherding industry—an occupation his listeners would have understood—to explain his special relationship with his people. The following facts about shepherding may give you added insight into Jesus' illustration.

1. Often, two journeying shepherds would bring their flocks together for the night. It was impossible for the two shepherds to keep their sheep separate, so in the morning when it was time to depart, one of the shepherds would stand some distance from the herd and begin calling out. His sheep, familiar with his voice, would run toward him, and soon his entire flock would be accounted for.

2. Sheepfolds in the sheep farmer's fields were usually crude corrals made of stacked stones. To protect the sheep and keep them in the fold at night, the shepherd would often lie across the entrance to the sheepfold.

Taking It Inward

Sheepyness Has Its Privileges

The Greek word for *listen* in John 10:27 is *akouo*. This word connotes more than hearing. It means, "to pay attention to." Anyone can hear Jesus' voice, but only his sheep pay attention. How's your attentiveness these days? Are you "hearing" what Jesus is saying? The questions that follow are tailored to you as a youth worker and spiritual leader. The questions you'll use with the group are slightly different.

Looking at your list of facts about sheep from John 10, what benefits do sheep receive?

Who or what is the shepherd of your life? In other words, where do you put your trust? Is it in...

- your pastor?
- denominational leaders?
- friends?
- a mentor?
- books or magazines about ministry?
- Christian authors or musicians?
- Jesus?
- something or someone else?

Jesus has sacrificed the most to be your shepherd, but what are some ways you're not allowing him to be your shepherd?

What steps can you take to change that?

Wrapping It Up

Before finishing up, select the appropriate Teach It guide for your session (full Teach It guides are on the CD-ROM accompanying this book). Then read through the guide so you're familiar with the flow of the session and confident with each exercise. Be sure to allow time for printing or photocopying student pages and pulling together any materials needed (see the Materials step in the Teach It guide).

It's possible that some of your students have never truly "heard" the good shepherd's voice so as to give it their full attention. Pray that they'll be open to the message of John 10 and see that the good shepherd is the only one who truly cares for them. That's why he alone can guarantee them abundant life.

WEB SUPPORT:
Remember to check out Web support for *See, Believe, Live* at www.inword.org. You'll find updated media suggestions (music, video clips), along with additional prep helps and even more application ideas. When at www.inword.org, look for the Digging Deeper series icon. You'll find password information in the Instructions at the front of this book.

John 10:1-42

1 "I tell you the truth, the man who does not enter the sheep pen by the gate, but climbs in by some other way, is a thief and a robber.

2 The man who enters by the gate is the shepherd of his sheep.

3 The watchman opens the gate for him, and the sheep listen to his voice. He calls his own sheep by name and leads them out.

4 When he has brought out all his own, he goes on ahead of them, and his sheep follow him because they know his voice.

5 But they will never follow a stranger; in fact, they will run away from him because they do not recognize a stranger's voice."

6 Jesus used this figure of speech, but they did not understand what he was telling them.

7 Therefore Jesus said again, "I tell you the truth, I am the gate for the sheep.

8 All who ever came before me were thieves and robbers, but the sheep did not listen to them.

9 I am the gate; whoever enters through me will be saved. He will come in and go out, and find pasture.

10 The thief comes only to steal and kill and destroy; I have come that they may have life, and have it to the full.

11 "I am the good shepherd. The good shepherd lays down his life for the sheep.

12 The hired hand is not the shepherd who owns the sheep. So when he sees the wolf coming, he abandons the sheep and runs away. Then the wolf attacks the flock and scatters it.

13 The man runs away because he is a hired hand and cares nothing for the sheep.

14 "I am the good shepherd; I know my sheep and my sheep know me—

15 just as the Father knows me and I know the Father—and I lay down my life for the sheep.

16 I have other sheep that are not of this sheep pen. I must bring them also. They too will listen to my voice, and there shall be one flock and one shepherd.

17 The reason my Father loves me is that I lay down my life—only to take it up again.

18 No one takes it from me, but I lay it down of my own accord. I have authority to lay it down and authority to take it up again. This command I received from my Father."

19 At these words the Jews were again divided.

20 Many of them said, "He is demon-possessed and raving mad. Why listen to him?"

21 But others said, "These are not the sayings of a man possessed by a demon. Can a demon open the eyes of the blind?"

22 Then came the Feast of Dedication at Jerusalem. It was winter,

23 and Jesus was in the temple area walking in Solomon's Colonnade.

24 The Jews gathered around him, saying, "How long will you keep us in suspense? If you are the Christ, tell us plainly."

25 Jesus answered, "I did tell you, but you do not believe. The miracles I do in my Father's name speak for me,

26 but you do not believe because you are not my sheep.

27 My sheep listen to my voice; I know them, and they follow me.

28 I give them eternal life, and they shall never perish; no one can snatch them out of my hand.

29 My Father, who has given them to me, is greater than all; no one can snatch them out of my Father's hand.

30 I and the Father are one."

31 Again the Jews picked up stones to stone him,

32 but Jesus said to them, "I have shown you many great miracles from the Father. For which of these do you stone me?"

33 "We are not stoning you for any of these," replied the Jews, "but for blasphemy, because you, a mere man, claim to be God."

34 Jesus answered them, "Is it not written in your Law, 'I have said you are gods'?

35 If he called them 'gods,' to whom the word of God came—and the Scripture cannot be broken—

36 what about the one whom the Father set apart as his very own and sent into the world? Why then do you accuse me of blasphemy because I said, 'I am God's Son'?

37 Do not believe me unless I do what my Father does.

38 But if I do it, even though you do not believe me, believe the miracles, that you may know and

understand that the Father is in me, and I in the Father."

39 Again they tried to seize him, but he escaped their grasp.

40 Then Jesus went back across the Jordan to the place where John had been baptizing in the early days. Here he stayed

41 and many people came to him. They said, "Though John never performed a miraculous sign, all that John said about this man was true."

42 And in that place many believed in Jesus.

1. Materials

For this session each student will need—
- the Session 7 Scripture sheet
- the student journal page for Session 7
- his or her own Bible, a pen, and a notebook

You'll also need—
- a whiteboard and markers
- a pack of colored pencils (at least two colors per student)
- sheep trivia

2. Session Intro

GOALS OF SESSION 7

As students experience this session, they will—
- discover that no one has more interest in their well-being than Jesus.
- see how they can experience abundant life when they pay attention to Jesus' voice.
- rearrange their lives to be in a better position to listen when Jesus speaks.

PRAYER

OPEN: *SHEEP FACTS*

Group Presentation: Play a trivia game to get students thinking about sheep.

3. Digging In: *What's a Metaphor? (To Keep the Sheep In)*

Group Dig: Explore John 10:1-18 to discover one of Jesus' greatest analogies in explaining his relationship with us.

4. Cross-Checking: *More on Sheep and Shepherds*

Personal Retreat: Ezekiel, of all people, gave us a great heads-up on Jesus' teaching.

5. Taking It Inward: *Perfect Gate, Perfect Shepherd*

Group Interaction: Bring Jesus' teachings and analogies into today's world.

6. Digging Deeper: *Be a Sheep!*

Group Dig: It's no accident why Jesus compared us to sheep. John 10:19-30 tells why.

7. Taking It Inward: *Sheepyness Has Its Privileges*

Group Interaction: Let students reflect on which "shepherd" they've been trusting the most.

8. Wrapping It Up: *Sheep Ears*

Challenge students to do something out of gratitude for the fact that the perfect shepherd laid down his life for them.

1. Materials

For this session each student will need—
- the Session 7 Scripture sheet
- the student journal page for Session 7
- his or her own Bible, a pen, and a notebook

You'll also need—
- a whiteboard and markers
- a pack of colored pencils (at least two colors per student)
- sheep trivia

2. Session Intro

GOALS OF SESSION 7

As students experience this session, they will—
- discover that no one has more interest in their well-being than Jesus.
- see how they can experience abundant life when they pay attention to Jesus' voice.
- rearrange their lives to be in a better position to listen when Jesus speaks.

PRAYER

OPEN: *SHEEP FACTS*
Group Presentation: Play a trivia game to get students thinking about sheep.

3. Digging In: *What's a Metaphor? (To Keep the Sheep In)*

Group Dig: Explore John 10:1-18 to discover one of Jesus' greatest analogies in explaining his relationship with us.

4. Cross-Checking: *More on Sheep and Shepherds*

Personal Retreat: Ezekiel, of all people, gave us a great heads-up on Jesus' teaching.

5. Taking It Inward: *Perfect Gate, Perfect Shepherd*

Group Interaction: Bring Jesus' teachings and analogies into today's world.

6. Digging Deeper: *Be a Sheep!*

Group Dig: It's no accident why Jesus compared us to sheep. John 10:19-30 tells why.

7. Taking It Inward: *Sheepyness Has Its Privileges*

Group Interaction: Let students reflect on which "shepherd" they've been trusting the most.

8. Wrapping It Up: *Sheep Ears*

Challenge students to do something out of gratitude for the fact that the perfect shepherd laid down his life for them.

1. Materials

For this session each student will need—
- the Session 7 Scripture sheet
- the student journal page for Session 7
- his or her own Bible, a pen, and a notebook

You'll also need—
- a whiteboard and markers
- a pack of colored pencils (at least two colors per student)
- sheep trivia on slips of paper

2. Session Intro

GOALS OF SESSION 7

As students experience this session, they will—
- discover that no one has more interest in their well-being than Jesus.
- see how they can experience abundant life when they pay attention to Jesus' voice.
- rearrange their lives to be in a better position to listen when Jesus speaks.

PRAYER

OPEN: *SHEEP FACTS*

Group Game: Play this Balderdash-style game with sheep trivia to get your students thinking about sheep.

3. Digging In: *What's a Metaphor? (To Keep the Sheep In)*

Group Dig: Explore John 10:1-18 to discover one of Jesus' greatest analogies in explaining his relationship with us.

4. Cross-Checking: *More on Sheep and Shepherds*

Personal Retreat: Jeremiah and Ezekiel gave us a great heads-up on Jesus' teaching.

5. Taking It Inward: *Perfect Gate, Perfect Shepherd*

Group Interaction: Bring Jeremiah's, Ezekiel's, and Jesus' teachings into today's world.

6. Digging Deeper: *Be a Sheep!*

Group Dig: It's no accident that Jesus compared us to sheep. John 10:19-30 tells why.

7. Taking It Inward: *Sheepyness Has Its Privileges*

Group Interaction: Let students reflect on which "shepherd" they've been trusting the most.

8. Wrapping It Up: *Sheep Ears*

Challenge students to do something out of gratitude for the fact that the perfect shepherd laid down his life for them.

1. Materials

For this session each student will need—
- the Session 7 Scripture sheet
- the student journal page for Session 7
- his or her own Bible, a pen, and a notebook

You'll also need—
- a whiteboard and markers
- a pack of colored pencils (at least two colors per student)
- sheep-trivia pop quiz

2. Session Intro

GOALS OF SESSION 7

As students experience this session, they will—
- discover that no one has more interest in their well-being than Jesus.
- see how they can experience abundant life when they pay attention to Jesus' voice.
- rearrange their lives to be in a better position to listen when Jesus speaks.

PRAYER

OPEN: *SHEEP FACTS*

Group Quiz: Open your session with a pop quiz on sheep trivia to get your students thinking about sheep.

3. Digging In: *What's a Metaphor? (To Keep the Sheep In)*

Group Dig: Explore John 10:1-18 to discover one of Jesus' greatest analogies in explaining his relationship with us.

4. Cross-Checking: *More on Sheep and Shepherds*

Personal Retreat: Jeremiah and Ezekiel gave us a great heads-up on Jesus' teaching.

5. Taking It Inward: *Perfect Gate, Perfect Shepherd*

Group Interaction: Bring Jeremiah's, Ezekiel's, and Jesus' teachings into today's world.

6. Digging Deeper: *Be a Sheep!*

Group Dig: It's no accident that Jesus compared us to sheep. John 10:19-30 tells why.

7. Taking It Inward: *Sheepyness Has Its Privileges*

Group Interaction: Let students reflect on which "shepherd" they've been trusting the most.

8. Wrapping It Up: *Sheep Ears*

Challenge students to do something out of gratitude for the fact that the perfect shepherd laid down his life for them.

1. Materials

For this session each student will need—

- his or her own Bible
- optional: the student journal page for Session 7 (Using the student journal page is optional in the coffeehouse setting since table space will be limited.)

You'll also need—

- optional: a copy of the sheep-trivia quiz
- a pack of pencils with erasers
- optional: a few spare Bibles for students who've forgotten theirs

2. Session Intro

GOALS OF SESSION 7

As students experience this session, they will—

- discover that no one has more interest in their well-being than Jesus.
- see how they can experience abundant life when they pay attention to Jesus' voice.
- rearrange their lives to be in a better position to listen when Jesus speaks.

PRAYER

OPEN: *SHEEP FACTS*

Group Game: Play this game with sheep trivia to get your students thinking about sheep.

3. Digging In: *What's a Metaphor? (To Keep the Sheep In)*

Group Dig: Explore John 10:1-18 to discover one of Jesus' greatest analogies in explaining his relationship with us.

4. Cross-Checking: *More on Sheep and Shepherds*

Group Dig: Ezekiel gave us a great heads-up on Jesus' teaching.

5. Taking It Inward: *Perfect Gate, Perfect Shepherd*

Group Interaction: Bring Jeremiah's, Ezekiel's, and Jesus' teachings into today's world.

6. Digging Deeper: *Be a Sheep!*

Group Dig: It's no accident that Jesus compared us to sheep. John 10:25-30 tells why.

7. Taking It Inward: *Sheepyness Has Its Privileges*

Group Interaction: Let students reflect on which "shepherd" they've been trusting the most.

8. Wrapping It Up: *Sheep Ears*

Challenge students to do something out of gratitude for the fact that the perfect shepherd laid down his life for them.

1. Materials (Optional)

- Movie Clip: scene from the movie *Hoosiers* in which Coach Norman Dale (Gene Hackman) gives a speech to his team at the Indiana regional finals: Chapter 25, "The Best you Can Be"—DVD counter cues, 1:15:45 to 1:17:20
- Demotivational Talk: Collect a few of your favorite "demotivator" sayings from www.despair.com/viewall.html to read to your students. Caution: You'll be tempted to spend the rest of your day perusing this site!
- Quotations representing different leadership needs

2. Optional Opens

Movie Clip: *Hoosiers*
Demotivational Talk: Read a few of your favorite "demotivators" from www.despair.com.
Quotations: quotations to introduce the subject of how to encourage and light fires under people.

3. Digging In

Personal Story: Share about a time when someone wanted the best for you and encouraged you to go to the next level.
God's Perspective: God wants the best for us.
Our Perspective: We want many things, but often we go after things that don't bring us life.
John 10:9-16

4. Taking It Inward

Analyze Jesus' sheep/shepherd illustration by considering:
- the thief
- the wolf
- the hired hand
- the good shepherd

5. Wrapping It Up

Challenge students to grow so close to Jesus they can recognize his voice throughout the day.

SESSION 8

JOHN 11
LET GO...LET GOD

Setting the Heart

In Ephesians 3, Paul voices a prayer on behalf of his fellow believers in Ephesus. He closes it with this benediction:

> Now to him who is able to do immeasurably more than all we ask or imagine, according to his power that is at work within us, to him be glory in the church and in Christ Jesus throughout all generations, for ever and ever! Amen. (Ephesians 3:20-21)

Consider this question: If God is able to do immeasurably more than *all* we ask or imagine—and he is—what then should be the focus of our prayers? Too often our prayers are more about what we want than what God wants. Yet God is able to do *immeasurably more* than what we want!

In John 11, Jesus' friends didn't hesitate in expressing what they wanted when they lost someone they deeply loved. But Jesus had much more in mind. Open your heart to the reality that God has your best interest in mind regarding *every* aspect of your life. Before you begin your personal prep, spend a few moments in prayer. Submit your desires to God's desires—and anticipate his immeasurably better response.

Digging In

Front-Row Seat at the Resurrection

The events of John 11 play out before three groups or individuals: the disciples, Martha, and a number of interested Jews. In this session, we'll look at these events through each party's eyes. First, let's glean all we can about these three groups or individuals. Then we'll put it all together.

THE DISCIPLES
Read John 11:1-17 using your Scripture sheet.

1. Mark every mention of the disciples with an "ichthus" .

2. Mark every mention of Jesus (including what he said and did) with a cross .

3. Mark every description of Lazarus' condition by circling it.

Now glance back at what you marked, and write your responses to these questions:

What was Lazarus' condition at the beginning of this passage?

What was his condition at the end of the passage?

From what Jesus said, why was Lazarus sick, and why did he die?

MARTHA
Now read John 11:17-30.

1. Mark every mention of Martha (including what she said and did) with a female stick figure .

2. Mark every mention of Jesus with a cross .

3. Mark the words *know* and *believe* (along with any forms of these words) with a light bulb .

Meditating on what you've marked, respond to these questions:

Do you see any change in Lazarus' condition in this segment of John 11?

What were the first words out of Martha's mouth when she saw Jesus?

What did Martha want?

What did Jesus want? (See John 11:14 and 15, and jot down his actual words.)

What did Martha *know* and *believe*?

THE JEWS AND JEWISH LEADERS
Finally, read John 11:31-48.

1. Mark every mention of the Jews and Jewish leaders with a Star of David .

2. Mark every mention of Jesus with a cross .

3. Mark the words *believe* and *know* with a light bulb .

Now record your answers to the following questions:

What was Lazarus' condition at the beginning of this passage?

What was his condition at the end?

What human traits did you observe in Jesus?

How did the Jews witnessing these events respond to Lazarus' resurrection?

How did the Jewish leaders handle the news of this miracle?

What were the Jewish leaders afraid of?

BEFORE YOU MOVE ON...
You may have noticed Jesus didn't reach Bethany until Lazarus had been in the tomb for four days. There is historic evidence that the Hebrew people believed that the spirit remained in the vicinity of a dead body for three days, departing to Sheol on the fourth. The fact that this miracle occurred after Lazarus had been dead for four days would have suggested to John's readers that a true resurrection—rather than a healing or resuscitation—had occurred.

Taking It Inward

"Lord, If You Would Just…"

Whew! You've uncovered a lot of information—time to let it sink in. Let the questions below help you apply John 11 to your "Lazarus situations."

What good resulted from the tragedy of Lazarus' death? (See John 11:45.)

Would this have happened had Martha received her short-term wish?

What "Lazarus situations" do you have going on in your life—challenging situations in which you're saying to God, as Martha did, "Lord, if you would just…"? List them here.

Cross-Checking

Perspective Is Everything

With these situations in mind, read the following passages from your Bible. Spend some time prayerfully meditating on these verses, and allow God to show you what he wants to accomplish through your "Lazarus situations." Under each verse reference, record anything you see that explains why we have "Lazarus situations." Also, keep your eyes peeled for anything that tells you how to handle these circumstances or what help you can expect from God.

Genesis 50:18-20
(The action picks up just after Joseph reveals his identity to his brothers in Egypt.)

John 9:3

John 11:4, 14-15

Romans 8:24-39

James 1:2-4

Now take a moment to apply these truths to your "Lazarus situations." It's likely that your feelings about these situations are similar to Martha's; you'd rather not have to contend with them. But what do these Scriptures say to you? In the space below, write a prayer reflecting the truth you've uncovered in this session.

Wrapping It Up

If You're Reading This, Something Went Wrong

Jesus is able to walk with you, weep with you, and strengthen you in whatever "Lazarus situations" you face. But the greatest help may lie in the fact that he's able to equip you with his perspective on what he wants to accomplish through these situations. And remember that in all of these things, Jesus is able to do *immeasurably more* than you can ask or even imagine (Ephesians 3:20).

Have you ever seen an action movie in which the hero got into a tight spot and popped in a tape or CD that said, "Well, if you're hearing these words, something must have gone wrong!"? Then the voice on the tape gives the guy a plan to help get him out of the jam. Take a minute to write down a truth from this session that can help you whenever something in your life goes wrong. Right now you may be sailing along with no problems. But a day will come when you'll need the encouragement of this session.

Select the appropriate Teach It guide for your session (full Teach It guides are on the CD-ROM accompanying this book). Then read through the guide so you're familiar with the flow of the session and confident with each exercise. Be sure to allow time for printing or photocopying student pages and pulling together any materials needed (see the Materials step in the Teach It guide). In the group session, your students won't cover the segment dealing with the disciples (John 11:1-17) in as much detail as you have here. As you read the Teach It guide, be sure to note the suggested options for handling this portion of John 11 with the group.

One more note: This session doesn't cover the last few verses of John 11. Be sure to read John 11:49-57 for yourself. After Jesus' resurrected Lazarus, the Jewish leaders' attitude toward Jesus changed; consequently, the events leading to his crucifixion were set in motion. These verses will help you see the dynamics of that change.

Spend a few moments praying for your students. Call to mind their names and faces, and pray they can experience through their hard life situations immeasurably more than they can ask or imagine.

WEB SUPPORT: Remember to check out Web support for *See, Believe, Live* at www.inword.org. You'll find updated media suggestions (music, video clips), along with additional prep helps and even more application ideas. When at www.inword.org, look for the Digging Deeper series icon. You'll find password information in the Instructions at the front of this book.

John 11:1-57

1   Now a man named Lazarus was sick. He was from Bethany, the village of Mary and her sister Martha.

2   This Mary, whose brother Lazarus now lay sick, was the same one who poured perfume on the Lord and wiped his feet with her hair.

3   So the sisters sent word to Jesus, "Lord, the one you love is sick."

4   When he heard this, Jesus said, "This sickness will not end in death. No, it is for God's glory so that God's Son may be glorified through it."

5   Jesus loved Martha and her sister and Lazarus.

6   Yet when he heard that Lazarus was sick, he stayed where he was two more days.

7   Then he said to his disciples, "Let us go back to Judea."

8   "But Rabbi," they said, "a short while ago the Jews tried to stone you, and yet you are going back there?"

9   Jesus answered, "Are there not twelve hours of daylight? A man who walks by day will not stumble, for he sees by this world's light.

10 It is when he walks by night that he stumbles, for he has no light."

11 After he had said this, he went on to tell them, "Our friend Lazarus has fallen asleep; but I am going there to wake him up."

12 His disciples replied, "Lord, if he sleeps, he will get better."

13 Jesus had been speaking of his death, but his disciples thought he meant natural sleep.

14 So then he told them plainly, "Lazarus is dead,

15 and for your sake I am glad I was not there, so that you may believe. But let us go to him."

16 Then Thomas (called Didymus) said to the rest of the disciples, "Let us also go, that we may die with him."

17 On his arrival, Jesus found that Lazarus had already been in the tomb for four days.

18 Bethany was less than two miles from Jerusalem,

19 and many Jews had come to Martha and Mary to comfort them in the loss of their brother.

20 When Martha heard that Jesus was coming, she went out to meet him, but Mary stayed at home.

21 "Lord," Martha said to Jesus, "if you had been here, my brother would not have died.

22 But I know that even now God will give you whatever you ask."

23 Jesus said to her, "Your brother will rise again."

24 Martha answered, "I know he will rise again in the resurrection at the last day."

25 Jesus said to her, "I am the resurrection and the life. He who believes in me will live, even though he dies;

26 and whoever lives and believes in me will never die. Do you believe this?"

27 "Yes, Lord," she told him, "I believe that you are the Christ, the Son of God, who was to come into the world."

28 And after she had said this, she went back and called her sister Mary aside. "The Teacher is here," she said, "and is asking for you."

29 When Mary heard this, she got up quickly and went to him.

30 Now Jesus had not yet entered the village, but was still at the place where Martha had met him.

31 When the Jews who had been with Mary in the house, comforting her, noticed how quickly she got up and went out, they followed her, supposing she was going to the tomb to mourn there.

32 When Mary reached the place where Jesus was and saw him, she fell at his feet and said, "Lord, if you had been here, my brother would not have died."

33 When Jesus saw her weeping, and the Jews who had come along with her also weeping, he was deeply moved in spirit and troubled.

34 "Where have you laid him?" he asked. "Come and see, Lord," they replied.

35 Jesus wept.

36 Then the Jews said, "See how he loved him!"

37 But some of them said, "Could not he who opened the eyes of the blind man have kept this man from dying?"

38 Jesus, once more deeply moved, came to the tomb. It was a cave with a stone laid across the entrance.

39 "Take away the stone," he said. "But, Lord," said Martha, the sister of the dead man, "by this time there is a bad odor, for he has been there four days."

40 Then Jesus said, "Did I not tell you that if you believed, you would see the glory of God?"

41 So they took away the stone. Then Jesus looked up and said, "Father, I thank you that you have heard me.

42 I knew that you always hear me, but I said this for the benefit of the people standing here, that they may believe that you sent me."

43 When he had said this, Jesus called in a loud voice, "Lazarus, come out!"

44 The dead man came out, his hands and feet wrapped with strips of linen, and a cloth around his face. Jesus said to them, "Take off the grave clothes and let him go."

45 Therefore many of the Jews who had come to visit Mary, and had seen what Jesus did, put their faith in him.

46 But some of them went to the Pharisees and told them what Jesus had done.

47 Then the chief priests and the Pharisees called a meeting of the Sanhedrin. "What are we accomplishing?" they asked. "Here is this man performing many miraculous signs.

48 If we let him go on like this, everyone will believe in him, and then the Romans will come and take away both our place and our nation."

49 Then one of them, named Caiaphas, who was high priest that year, spoke up, "You know nothing at all!

50 You do not realize that it is better for you that one man die for the people than that the whole nation perish."

51 He did not say this on his own, but as high priest that year he prophesied that Jesus would die for the Jewish nation,

52 and not only for that nation but also for the scattered children of God, to bring them together and make them one.

53 So from that day on they plotted to take his life.

54 Therefore Jesus no longer moved about publicly among the Jews. Instead he withdrew to a region near the desert, to a village called Ephraim, where he stayed with his disciples.

55 When it was almost time for the Jewish Passover, many went up from the country to Jerusalem for their ceremonial cleansing before the Passover.

56 They kept looking for Jesus, and as they stood in the temple area they asked one another, "What do you think? Isn't he coming to the Feast at all?"

57 But the chief priests and Pharisees had given orders that if anyone found out where Jesus was, he should report it so that they might arrest him.

1. Materials

For this session each student will need—
- the Session 8 Scripture sheet
- the student journal page for Session 8
- the Setting the Stage handout
- his or her own Bible, a pen, and a notebook

You'll also need—
- a whiteboard and markers
- a pack of colored pencils (at least three colors per student)
- optional movie clip: *Bridge to Terabithia*. Scene: funeral (Chapter 13—counter cues, 1:13:10 to 1:16:45)

2. Session Intro

GOALS OF SESSION 8

As students experience this session, they will—
- see the miracle of Lazarus' resurrection through the eyes of those who witnessed it.
- compare their feelings about difficult or unfair situations with Martha's feelings about her brother's death.
- seek God's perspective on the challenging circumstances they're facing now—or will face in life.

PRAYER

OPEN: *WHY DO THEY CALL IT A FUNERAL? (WHEN IT SURE ISN'T FUN)*
Video Clip: Use the funeral scene from the movie *Bridge to Terabithia* to set up John 11.

3. Pre-Dig: *Setting the Stage*

Reading Drama: This impromptu drama will let students see the action in John 11:1-16.

4. Digging In: *Front-Row Seat at the Resurrection*

Group Dig: Explore John 11:17-30 to look into the interaction between Jesus and Martha.

5. Digging Deeper: *Curious Crowd*

Group Dig: Explore John 11:31-48 from the crowd's perspective.

6. Taking It Inward: *"Lord, If You Would Just..."*

Group Interaction: Students will examine their own "Lazarus situations."

7. Cross-Checking: *Perspective Is Everything*

Group Read: Students will see what Genesis and Romans have to say about their "Lazarus situations."

8. Wrapping It Up: *If You're Reading This, Something Went Wrong*

Challenge students to bring the action of John 11 into their lives.

1. Materials

For this session each student will need—
- the Session 8 Scripture sheet
- the student journal page for Session 8
- the Setting the Stage handout
- his or her own Bible, a pen, and a notebook

You'll also need—
- a whiteboard and markers
- a pack of colored pencils (at least three colors per student)

2. Session Intro

GOALS OF SESSION 8

As students experience this session, they will—
- see the miracle of Lazarus' resurrection through the eyes of those who witnessed it.
- compare their feelings about difficult or unfair situations with Martha's feelings about her brother's death.
- seek God's perspective on the challenging circumstances they're facing now—or will face in life.

PRAYER

OPEN: *WHY DID HE WEEP?*
Lead with a brainstorm discussion on the Bible's shortest verse, "Jesus wept" (John 11:35).

3. Pre-Dig: *Setting the Stage*

Reading Drama: This impromptu drama will let students see the action in John 11:1-16.

4. Digging In: *Front-Row Seat at the Resurrection*

Group Dig: Explore John 11:17-30 to look into the interaction between Jesus and Martha.

5. Digging Deeper: *Curious Crowd*

Group Dig: Explore John 11:31-48 from the crowd's perspective.

6. Taking It Inward: *"Lord, If You Would Just..."*

Group Interaction: Students will examine their own "Lazarus situations."

7. Cross-Checking: *Perspective Is Everything*

Group Read: Students will see what Genesis and Romans have to say about their "Lazarus situations."

8. Wrapping It Up: *If You're Reading This, Something Went Wrong*

Challenge students to bring the action of John 11 into their lives.

1. Materials

For this session each student will need—
- the Session 8 Scripture sheet
- the student journal page for Session 8
- optional: the Setting the Stage handout
- his or her own Bible, a pen, and a notebook

You'll also need—
- a whiteboard and markers
- a pack of colored pencils (at least three colors per student)

2. Session Intro

GOALS OF SESSION 8

As students experience this session, they will—
- see the miracle of Lazarus' resurrection through the eyes of those who witnessed it.
- compare their feelings about difficult or unfair situations with Martha's feelings about her brother's death.
- seek God's perspective on the challenging circumstances they're facing now—or will face in life.

PRAYER

OPEN: *WHY DID HE WEEP?*
Lead with a brainstorm discussion on the Bible's shortest verse, "Jesus wept" (John 11:35).

3. Pre-Dig: *Setting the Stage*

Option 1: This impromptu drama will let students see the action in John 11:1-16.
Option 2: Use a group reading of John 11:1-16 for students to experience the action in these verses.

4. Digging In: *Front-Row Seat at the Resurrection*

Group Dig: Explore John 11:17-30 to look into the interaction between Jesus and Martha.

5. Digging Deeper: *Curious Crowd*

Group Dig: Explore John 11:31-48 from the crowd's perspective.

6. Taking It Inward: *"Lord, If You Would Just..."*

Group Interaction: Students will examine their own "Lazarus situations."

7. Cross-Checking: *Perspective Is Everything*

Personal Retreat: Students will see what several passages have to say about their "Lazarus situations."

8. Wrapping It Up: *If You're Reading This, Something Went Wrong*

Challenge students to bring the action of John 11 into their lives.

1. Materials

For this session each student will need—
- the Session 8 Scripture sheet
- the student journal page for Session 8
- his or her own Bible, a pen, and a notebook

You'll also need—
- a whiteboard and markers
- a pack of colored pencils (at least three colors per student)

2. Session Intro

GOALS OF SESSION 8

As students experience this session, they will—
- see the miracle of Lazarus' resurrection through the eyes of those who witnessed it.
- compare their feelings about difficult or unfair situations with Martha's feelings about her brother's death.
- seek God's perspective on the challenging circumstances they're facing now—or will face in life.

PRAYER

OPEN: *WHY DID HE WEEP?*
Lead with a brainstorm discussion on the Bible's shortest verse, "Jesus wept" (John 11:35).

3. Pre-Dig: *Setting the Stage*

Group Reading: Use a group reading of John 11:1-16 for students to experience the action in these verses.

4. Digging In: *Front-Row Seat at the Resurrection*

Group Dig: Explore John 11:17-30 to look into the interaction between Jesus and Martha.

5. Digging Deeper: *Curious Crowd*

Group Dig: Explore John 11:31-48 from the crowd's perspective.

6. Taking It Inward: *"Lord, If You Would Just..."*

Group Interaction: Students will examine their own "Lazarus situations."

7. Cross-Checking: *Perspective Is Everything*

Group Dig: Students will see what several passages have to say about their "Lazarus situations."

8. Wrapping It Up: *If You're Reading This, Something Went Wrong*

Challenge students to bring the action of John 11 into their lives.

1. Materials

For this session each student will need—
- his or her own Bible
- optional: the student journal page for Session 8 (Using the student journal page is optional in the coffeehouse setting since table space will be limited.)

You'll also need—
- a pack of pencils with erasers
- optional: a few spare Bibles for students who've forgotten theirs

2. Session Intro

GOALS OF SESSION 8

As students experience this session, they will—
- see the miracle of Lazarus' resurrection through the eyes of those who witnessed it.
- compare their feelings about difficult or unfair situations with Martha's feelings about her brother's death.
- seek God's perspective on the challenging circumstances they're facing now—or will face in life.

PRAYER

OPEN: *WHY DID HE WEEP?*
Lead with a brainstorm discussion on the Bible's shortest verse, "Jesus wept" (John 11:35).

3. Pre-Dig: *Setting the Stage*

Group Dig: Explore John 11:1-16 for students to experience the action in these verses.

4. Digging In: *Front-Row Seat at the Resurrection*

Group Dig: Explore John 11:17-30 to look into the interaction between Jesus and Martha.

5. Digging Deeper: *Curious Crowd*

Group Dig: Explore John 11:31-48 from the crowd's perspective.

6. Taking It Inward: *"Lord, If You Would Just..."*

Group Interaction: Students will examine their own "Lazarus situations."

7. Cross-Checking: *Perspective Is Everything*

Group Dig: Students will see what Genesis and Romans have to say about their "Lazarus situations."

8. Wrapping It Up: *If You're Reading This, Something Went Wrong*

Challenge students to bring the action of John 11 into their lives.

1. Materials (Optional)

- Movie Clip: *Rocky III*. Scene: Rocky Balboa's training: Chapter 13, "Getting Strong"— DVD counter cues, 1:15:22 to 1:18:47
- Pruning shears and something to cut, such as a twig or a pencil
- Quotations to introduce the idea that pain could be a good thing

2. Optional Opens

Movie Clip: *Rocky III*
Visual Illustration: pruning shears to help illustrate that pain can sometimes be a good thing
Quotations: notable quotations that teach us about the benefits of painful experiences

3. Digging In

Personal Story: Share about a time when pain turned out to be a good thing.
John 11:15
John 11:45

4. Taking It Inward

Is it possible that God can use the pain in our lives for something good?

5. Wrapping It Up

Challenge students to examine the painful situations in life to find the possible benefits.

SESSION 9

Setting the Heart

If it's been a while since you've been in John 12, how about giving it a quick read before jumping into today's study of John 13? Unique to John's writing is that he recorded Jesus' triumphant, pre-crucifixion entry into Jerusalem near the halfway point of his Gospel—John 12. (The other Gospel writers saved this event for the closing chapters of theirs.) So from John 13 on, we'll look at the final few days of Jesus' ministry on earth. To prepare your heart, read the verses below—poignant words from Jesus' final public teaching.

> Jesus replied, "The hour has come for the Son of Man to be glorified. I tell you the truth, unless a kernel of wheat falls to the ground and dies, it remains only a single seed. But if it dies, it produces many seeds. The man who loves his life will lose it, while the man who hates his life in this world will keep it for eternal life. Whoever serves me must follow me; and where I am, my servant also will be. My Father will honor the one who serves me. Now my heart is troubled, and what shall I say? 'Father, save me from this hour'? No, it was for this very reason I came to this hour." (John 12:23-27)

Digging In

Read the Red

Open up a red-letter edition of the Bible, and you'll notice that John 13–17 is a sea of red ink. It looks like one long monologue from Jesus—and for the most part, it is. This passage recounts the most critical and intense conversation between Jesus and the disciples recorded in John's Gospel—a conversation full of information and assurances that would prepare them to continue Jesus' work after his departure.

Jesus set the stage for this historic conversation with an historic action.

Read John 13:1-17 from your Scripture sheet. As you read—

1. Draw a clock 🕐 over words or phrases that refer to time or God's "divine clock." (You'll know what this means when you see it.)

2. Use a different color to underline anything Jesus *did*.

3. Use a third color to circle anything Jesus *said* about what he was doing (e.g., an explanation, teaching, or instruction).

What did you learn from marking references to time in this passage?

Look at what you underlined in John 13:4-5. Record below a play-by-play account of what Jesus *did*.

1.

2.

3.

4.

5.
6.

Now list everything Jesus *said* about what he did. Be sure to note any promises or instructions.

How would you summarize the significance of what Jesus did in this scene?

What is significant about the timing of the act?

Did you notice how John describes this action in verse 1? Write John's words below.

Digging Deeper

Show and Tell

Shortly after Jesus *showed* his disciples the full extent of his love, he *taught* them about love. Just think: The disciples had already experienced one of the greatest object lessons of all time. While the experience was still fresh in their memories, Jesus gave a specific command; then he attached several vital facts to that command.

Read John 13:31-38 using your Scripture sheet. Look for the answers to the questions below. When you find the info in Scripture, underline it. Then record it in the space provided.

What did Jesus command?

To what extent are we to obey this command?

What will result if and when we obey this command?

Taking It Inward

The Love Connection

Meditate for a moment on Jesus' "new command," and write your responses to the following questions.

Who is it that Jesus' disciples are to love?

How does this compare with other groups of people we're commanded to love? Off the top of your head, jot down two or three other groups Scripture tells us to love. If you're drawing a blank, check out Matthew 5:44, Matthew 22:37-39, and Luke 6:32-35.

At this point in Jesus' ministry, what example did the disciples have to go on when Jesus told them to love as he had loved them?

In your opinion, why is there such a strong connection between Christians loving each other and the world seeing us as Jesus' disciples?

Insight

A Little Greek

LOVE

Jesus said, "As I have loved you, so you must love one another." In the ancient Greek language, there were three common words for *love*:

> **agapao**—This word, used in John 13:34, conveys a sacrificial love—a love not based on the recipient's worthiness, but on the attitude of the one who bestows it. It's the type of love God expressed toward mankind in Jesus Christ and the love he desires among his children, one toward the other. *Agapao* love is an "I want the best for you" kind of love. (See 1 Corinthians 13 to learn how this type of love is lived out in relationships.)

> **phileo**—This word expresses friendship or brotherly love between relatives or friends. In teenager verbiage, it's a "let's go to the mall together" type of love.

> **eros**—The Greeks used this word to describe the romantic love between a man and a woman. It doesn't appear in the New Testament.[4]

DISCIPLE

The Greek word for *disciple* is *mathetes*, which means "learner."[5] In Jesus' day, disciples followed their teachers for the express purpose of becoming like them. The goal of discipleship was that the learners' lives would reflect the teacher's character traits and teachings. With love being so integral to Jesus' character and ministry, the disciples in turn were to model their teacher by loving one another as Jesus loved them.

Cross-Checking

The Look of Love

Other verses in God's Word have much to teach us about Jesus' command to love one another. Read the following passages (each of which uses a form of the word *agapao*) from your Bible. As you read, consider the questions in the chart headings, and write down your responses. You won't find answers for each question in every verse.

---

4 Lawrence O. Richards, *Expository Dictionary of Bible Words* (Grand Rapids: Zondervan Publishing House, 1985), 420.
5 Richards, 226.

	What commands to love do you see?	To what degree are we to love?	What results can we expect when we love this way?
Ephesians 4:32–5:2			
1 Thessalonians 4:9-12			
1 John 4:10-16			

Now take a few minutes to meditate on the truths you've uncovered. Let these questions guide your response to the impressions God has placed on your heart:

Think about the current state of your church and student ministry. Just by observing the love between people in your church and student ministry ("each other"), can the world easily tell you're Jesus' disciples?

Who in your church or student ministry have you not loved as Christ loved you? (If other people may be reading your notes, feel free to write in code.) Whose feet do you need to wash?

Believers often dismiss Jesus' command to love as he loved as lofty and unattainable. In fact, when 1 Corinthians 13 is taught, it's often presented as a divine ideal that's impossible for mere mortals to practice! But think for a minute. When Jesus commanded the disciples, "Love one another as I have loved you," he hadn't yet died on the cross. But what, in fact, had he just done? What does this teach you about how possible it is to "love as Jesus loved"?

Wrapping It Up

The Lock of Love

The purpose of the group session is to help your students understand Jesus' teaching and consider how they can love one another sacrificially. Select the appropriate Teach It guide for your session (full Teach It guides are on the CD-ROM accompanying this book). Then read through it so you're familiar with the flow of the session and confident with each exercise. Be sure to allow time for printing or photocopying student pages and pulling together any materials needed (see the Materials step in the Teach It guide).

EXERCISE HEADS-UP: All the Session 11 Teach It guides (except Coffeehouse and Talk) contain a closing option of taking communion as a group, which will take some extra prep. You may want to look at that option now if you're using those guides.

WEB SUPPORT: Remember to check out Web support for *See, Believe, Live* at www.inword.org. You'll find updated media suggestions (music, video clips), along with additional prep helps and even more application ideas. When at www.inword.org, look for the Digging Deeper series icon. You'll find password information in the Instructions at the front of this book.

Finally, you won't cover John 13:18-30 in the group session. As the leader, you should go ahead and read these verses to enrich your understanding of the chapter.

Before you close your book, take a minute to pray for your students—that their hearts will be softened to what God wants to show them about loving one another.

John 13:1-38

1 It was just before the Passover Feast. Jesus knew that the time had come for him to leave this world and go to the Father. Having loved his own who were in the world, he now showed them the full extent of his love.

2 The evening meal was being served, and the devil had already prompted Judas Iscariot, son of Simon, to betray Jesus.

3 Jesus knew that the Father had put all things under his power, and that he had come from God and was returning to God;

4 so he got up from the meal, took off his outer clothing, and wrapped a towel around his waist.

5 After that, he poured water into a basin and began to wash his disciples' feet, drying them with the towel that was wrapped around him.

6 He came to Simon Peter, who said to him, "Lord, are you going to wash my feet?"

7 Jesus replied, "You do not realize now what I am doing, but later you will understand."

8 "No," said Peter, "you shall never wash my feet." Jesus answered, "Unless I wash you, you have no part with me."

9 "Then, Lord," Simon Peter replied, "not just my feet but my hands and my head as well!"

10 Jesus answered, "A person who has had a bath needs only to wash his feet; his whole body is clean. And you are clean, though not every one of you."

11 For he knew who was going to betray him, and that was why he said not every one was clean.

12 When he had finished washing their feet, he put on his clothes and returned to his place. "Do you understand what I have done for you?" he asked them.

13 "You call me 'Teacher' and 'Lord,' and rightly so, for that is what I am.

14 Now that I, your Lord and Teacher, have washed your feet, you also should wash one another's feet.

15 I have set you an example that you should do as I have done for you.

16 I tell you the truth, no servant is greater than his master, nor is a messenger greater than the one who sent him.

17 Now that you know these things, you will be blessed if you do them.

18 "I am not referring to all of you; I know those I have chosen. But this is to fulfill the scripture: 'He who shares my bread has lifted up his heel against me.'

19 "I am telling you now before it happens, so that when it does happen you will believe that I am He.

20 I tell you the truth, whoever accepts anyone I send accepts me; and whoever accepts me accepts the one who sent me."

21 After he had said this, Jesus was troubled in spirit and testified, "I tell you the truth, one of you is going to betray me."

22 His disciples stared at one another, at a loss to know which of them he meant.

23 One of them, the disciple whom Jesus loved, was reclining next to him.

24 Simon Peter motioned to this disciple and said, "Ask him which one he means."

25 Leaning back against Jesus, he asked him, "Lord, who is it?"

26 Jesus answered, "It is the one to whom I will give this piece of bread when I have dipped it in the dish." Then, dipping the piece of bread, he gave it to Judas Iscariot, son of Simon.

27 As soon as Judas took the bread, Satan entered into him. "What you are about to do, do quickly," Jesus told him,

28 but no one at the meal understood why Jesus said this to him.

29 Since Judas had charge of the money, some thought Jesus was telling him to buy what was needed for the Feast, or to give something to the poor.

30 As soon as Judas had taken the bread, he went out. And it was night.

31 When he was gone, Jesus said, "Now is the Son of Man glorified and God is glorified in him.

32 If God is glorified in him, God will glorify the Son in himself, and will glorify him at once.

33 "My children, I will be with you only a little longer. You will look for me, and just as I told the Jews, so I tell you now: Where I am going, you cannot come.

34 "A new command I give you: Love one another. As I have loved you, so you must love one another.

35 By this all men will know that you are my disciples, if you love one another."

36 Simon Peter asked him, "Lord, where are you going?" Jesus replied, "Where I am going, you cannot follow now, but you will follow later."

37 Peter asked, "Lord, why can't I follow you now? I will lay down my life for you."

38 Then Jesus answered, "Will you really lay down your life for me? I tell you the truth, before the rooster crows, you will disown me three times!

1. Materials

For this session each student will need—
- the Session 9 Scripture sheet
- the student journal page for Session 9
- his or her own Bible, a pen, and a notebook

You'll also need—
- a whiteboard and markers
- a pack of colored pencils (at least two colors per student)
- optional: Search a video-sharing Web site with key words such as *howling dog* and *I love you*. You're sure to find a clip of a dog howling the phrase, "I love you."
- optional: one candy bar or granola bar for each student
- optional: buckets or basins, towels, and plenty of warm water (See the Optional Close in Wrapping It Up.)

2. Session Intro

GOALS OF SESSION 9
As students experience this session, they will—
- gain an understanding of Jesus' command to sacrificially love one another.
- examine their hearts for any deficiencies in showing sacrificial love.
- discuss practical ways to live out this kind of love.

PRAYER

OPEN: *RUH-ROH LOVE LANGUAGE*
Video Clip: Use this video clip to see love spoken in a whole new language.

3. Digging In: *Read the Red*

Group Dig: Explore John 13:1-17 to see what Jesus did and to see what Jesus said about what he did.

4. Digging Deeper: *Show and Tell*

Group Dig: Put the *Who? What?* and *How?* questions to John 13:31-35.

5. Taking It Inward: *The Love Connection*

Group Interaction: Process the implications of just exactly whom Jesus told us to love.

6. Cross-Checking: *The Look of Love*

Personal Retreat: Let 1 Thessalonians and 1 John add some insight into Jesus-grade love.

7. Wrapping It Up: *The Lock of Love*

Object Lesson: Use a candy bar or granola bar as incentive to put a plan of action into place for loving as Jesus loved.

Optional Close: Take Jesus literally and wash each other's feet, either during your session or scheduled during another time. Let this be a first act of love.

1. Materials

For this session each student will need—
- the Session 9 Scripture sheet
- the student journal page for Session 9
- his or her own Bible, a pen, and a notebook

You'll also need—
- a whiteboard and markers
- a pack of colored pencils (at least two colors per student)
- optional: Search a video-sharing Web site with key words such as *howling dog* and *I love you*. You're sure to find a clip of a dog howling the phrase, "I love you."
- optional: buckets or basins, towels, and plenty of warm water (See the Optional Close in Wrapping It Up.)

2. Session Intro

GOALS OF SESSION 9
As students experience this session, they will—
- gain an understanding of Jesus' command to sacrificially love one another.
- examine their hearts for any deficiencies in showing sacrificial love.
- discuss practical ways to live out this kind of love.

PRAYER

OPEN: *RUH-ROH LOVE LANGUAGE*
Video Clip: Use this video clip to see love spoken in a whole new language.

3. Digging In: *Read the Red*

Group Dig: Explore John 13:1-17 to see what Jesus did and to see what Jesus said about what he did.

4. Digging Deeper: *Show and Tell*

Group Dig: Put the *Who?* *What?* and *How?* questions to John 13:31-35 using a quiz.

5. Taking It Inward: *The Love Connection*

Group Interaction: Process the implications of just exactly whom Jesus told us to love.

6. Cross-Checking: *The Look of Love*

Personal Retreat: Let 1 Thessalonians and 1 John add some insight into Jesus-grade love.

7. Wrapping It Up: *The Lock of Love*

Challenge: Encourage students to think of a specific, practical act to show Jesus-grade love to someone.

Optional Close: Take Jesus literally and wash each other's feet, either during your session or scheduled during another time. Let this be a first act of love.

1. Materials

For this session each student will need—
- the Session 9 Scripture sheet
- the student journal page for Session 9
- his or her own Bible, a pen, and a notebook

You'll also need—
- a whiteboard and markers
- a pack of colored pencils (at least three colors per student)
- a red-letter edition of the Bible
- optional: Search a video-sharing Web site with key words such as *howling dog* and *I love you*. You're sure to find a clip of a dog howling the phrase, "I love you."
- optional: buckets or basins, towels, and warm water (See the Optional Close in Wrapping It Up.)

2. Session Intro

GOALS OF SESSION 9
As students experience this session, they will—
- gain an understanding of Jesus' command to sacrificially love one another.
- examine their hearts for any deficiencies in showing sacrificial love.
- discuss practical ways to live out this kind of love.

PRAYER

OPEN: *RUH-ROH LOVE LANGUAGE*
Video Clip: Use this video clip to see love spoken in a whole new language.

3. Digging In: *Read the Red*

Group Dig: Explore John 13:1-17 to see what Jesus did and to see what Jesus said about what he did.

4. Digging Deeper: *Show and Tell*

Group Dig: Put the *Who? What?* and *How?* questions to John 13:31-35.

5. Taking It Inward: *The Love Connection*

Group Interaction: Process the implications of just exactly whom Jesus told us to love.

6. Cross-Checking: *The Look of Love*

Personal Retreat: Let these New Testament passages add some insight into Jesus-grade love.

7. Wrapping It Up: *The Lock of Love*

Challenge: Encourage students to think of a specific, practical act to show Jesus-grade love to someone.

Optional Close: Take Jesus literally and wash each other's feet, either during your session or scheduled during another time. Let this be a first act of love.

1. Materials

For this session each student will need—
- the Session 9 Scripture sheet
- the student journal page for Session 9
- his or her own Bible, a pen, and a notebook

You'll also need—
- a whiteboard and markers
- a pack of colored pencils (at least three colors per student)
- optional: the NOOMA video, *Flame* (11 minutes). If you don't have this video, you can purchase the DVD from www.nooma.com.
- optional: Search a video-sharing Web site with key words such as howling dog and I love you. You're sure to find a clip of a dog howling the phrase, "I love you."
- optional: buckets or basins, towels, and plenty of warm water (See the Optional Close in Wrapping It Up.)
- optional: the movie trailer for *Pay It Forward*. You can play it from the DVD, or it may be available online at http://trailers.warnerbros.com/web/play.jsp?trailer=pay_it_for-ward_trailer. View the trailer before your session to make sure it's appropriate for your group.
- optional: the book, *Random Acts of Kindness*

2. Session Intro

GOALS OF SESSION 9
As students experience this session, they will—
- gain an understanding of Jesus' command to sacrificially love one another.
- examine their hearts for any deficiencies in showing sacrificial love.
- discuss practical ways to live out this kind of love.

PRAYER

OPEN:
Option 1: *Fi-uh (Southern Speak for "Fire")*
Video Clip: Open by showing the NOOMA video, *Flame*.

Option 2: *Ruh-Roh Love Language*
Video Clip: Use this video clip to see love spoken in a whole new language.

3. Digging In: *Read the Red*

Group Dig: Explore John 13:1-17 to see what Jesus did and to see what Jesus said about what he did.

4. Digging Deeper: *Show and Tell*

Group Dig: Put the *Who?* *What?* and *How?* questions to John 13:31-35.

5. Taking It Inward: *The Love Connection*

Group Interaction: Process the implications of just exactly whom Jesus told us to love.

6. Cross-Checking: *The Look of Love*

Personal Retreat: Let these New Testament passages add some insight into Jesus-grade love.

7. Wrapping It Up: *The Lock of Love*

Video Clip: Use the movie trailer from *Pay It Forward* to challenge students to think of a specific, practical act to show Jesus-grade love to someone.
Optional Close: Take Jesus literally and wash each other's feet, either during your session or scheduled during another time. Let this be a first act of love.

JOHN 13
SOLE MATES

1. Materials

For this session each student will need—
- his or her own Bible
- optional: the student journal page for Session 9 (Using the student journal page is optional in the coffeehouse setting since table space will be limited.)

You'll also need—
- optional: Internet access and a YouTube clip of a dog howling, "I love you"
- laptop
- a pack of pencils with erasers
- optional: a few spare Bibles for students who've forgotten theirs
- a red-letter edition of the Bible

2. Session Intro

GOALS OF SESSION 9
As students experience this session, they will—
- gain an understanding of Jesus' command to sacrificially love one another.
- examine their hearts for any deficiencies in showing sacrificial love.
- discuss practical ways to live out this kind of love.

PRAYER

OPEN: *RUH-ROH LOVE LANGUAGE*
Video Clip: Use this video clip to see love spoken in a whole new language.

3. Digging In: *Read the Red*

Group Dig: Explore John 13:1-17 to see what Jesus did and to see what Jesus said about what he did.

4. Digging Deeper: *Show and Tell*

Group Dig: Put the *Who? What?* and *How?* questions to John 13:31-35 in pop-quiz fashion.

5. Taking It Inward: *The Love Connection*

Group Interaction: Process the implications of just exactly whom Jesus told us to love.

6. Cross-Checking: *The Look of Love*

Group Dig: Let this 1 Thessalonians passage add some insight into Jesus-grade love.

7. Wrapping It Up: *The Lock of Love*

Challenge students to think of a specific, practical act to show Jesus-grade love to someone.

1. Materials (Optional)

- Video Clips: Choose two or three video clips from a video-sharing Web site that show historic achievements of people who did the impossible. Search words and phrases such as *Wright Brothers first powered flight*, *Roger Bannister breaking four-minute mile*, and *first man on the moon*. These clips will help illustrate the point (toward the end of the talk) that "love as Jesus loved" kind of love may seem hard to achieve, but when we do, it results in more people wanting more of this love.
- Quotations: famous people commenting on loving others

2. Optional Opens

Video Clips: Show clips of historic achievements of people who did the impossible.
Quotations: Introduce the idea of loving others with famous people commenting on loving others.
Story: Tell about someone who accomplished a seemingly impossible feat.

3. Digging In

John 13:34-37
God's Perspective: The only proof that you're following Christ is the way you love others.
Our Perspective: It might be easier to just wear the Christian T-shirt, but if we love others the way Jesus loved, people will want what we have.

4. Taking It Inward

Loving as Jesus loved doesn't come naturally, just like the feats witnessed in the opening videos.

5. Wrapping It Up

Challenge students to identify someone they can love as Jesus loved—and to go do it.

SESSION 10

Setting the Heart

As we saw in Session 9, when you leaf through a red-letter edition of the Bible, you find that John 14–17 is a sea of red ink. This part of Scripture looks like one long monologue from Jesus—and in reality, it is. Throughout this session, we'll examine aspects of this monologue as we explore one of Jesus' most critical and intense conversations with his disciples—a conversation full of teaching, assurances, and commands to help us live out our faith in a fallen world.

Several times during the course of this conversation, Jesus tells his disciples *why* it's necessary that he have this talk with them. The instance below sums it up the best.

> "All this I have told you so that you will not go astray... I have told you these things, so that in me you may have peace. In this world you will have trouble. But take heart! I have overcome the world." (John 16:1, 33)

Digging In

Words to Live By

Time was short. And Jesus had a lot to get across to his disciples—teachings they (and we) would need to go the distance with him.

Let's dive into these teachings by reading John 14:1-14 from the Scripture sheet.

> As you read, mark every mention of Jesus with a cross 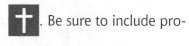. Be sure to include pronouns such as *I* and *my*.

Now look back at the crosses you marked. List below Jesus' major points about himself.

What promises does Jesus make in John 14:12-14? Record these below.

Cross-Checking

Did He Say "Greater"?

Take a second to read over the promises you just listed—some unbelievable promises (almost *too* unbelievable)! Maybe you're thinking, *Nah, it's impossible for me to do greater things than Jesus.* But before you start explaining away the promises Jesus intended *for you,* read the next set of passages. Look for any clues that indicate how you might actually do "greater things" than Jesus did. Here's a hint: Think beyond doing more miracles than Jesus did. You may recall from John's earlier writing that Jesus' miracles were merely "signs" meant to point people toward the greater works he came to earth to do—namely, to rescue us by way of his death and resurrection.

John 14:12
What's required of us before we can do greater works than Jesus did?

What would make this possible? (Look for where Jesus was going.)

Acts 1:1-8
When was the work of the apostles officially to begin? (What were they to wait for?)

How is that work defined in verse 8?

Acts 2:32-41
What facts were the disciples witnesses to? Detail them below.

What was the effect of their witness?

Based on what you've observed, what "greater things" are Christians—beginning with the apostles—to be doing as a result of Jesus' death, resurrection, and ascension, as well as the coming of the Holy Spirit?

Digging Deeper

Bold Claims, Bold Actions

In today's culture of relativism, John 14:6 is like a lightning rod. "How can you say that Jesus is *the* way, *the* truth, and *the* life?" the person with no absolutes might demand. "We each have our own path—our own journey to truth and to God!" There may be students in your group who have asked these very questions. If not, their friends undoubtedly have. The purpose of this session isn't to justify how or why Jesus is the way to God, but to give students an opportunity to *experience* him as the way to God.

Read the following verses, which show Jesus as the way, the truth, and the life. Detail in your notes how these passages relate to Jesus' claims in John 14.

John 8:28-32
What actions does Jesus ask of his listeners?

How do these actions connect with Jesus' claims? (Look for the word *then*.)

John 10:7-15

Colossians 2:1-10

How is Jesus able to make such bold claims in John 14? Think about Jesus as the way, the truth, and the life. Ask the Spirit of God to teach you about this, and write down what he reveals to your mind about Jesus in these roles.

Jesus as the Way	Jesus as the Truth	Jesus as the Life

Taking It Inward

Taking Jesus at His Word

Look back over all you've uncovered in Scripture today. Then write your responses to the questions below. (But wait! Don't start writing until you've really evaluated what we've covered thus far.)

What connections do you see between what Jesus said about himself and the promises he gave?

What does it appear that Jesus wants his disciples—you included—to grasp?

Jesus gave away the store to those who believe the truths he shared about himself. *We get it all!* But remember the prerequisite: We must believe in him. In the passages you've read in this session, Jesus gives some specific actions that will reveal your level of belief. Write down any that come to mind in the space below. If you need a refresher, check out John 8:28-32 and 14:12.

Have you tried to have it both ways—embracing a watered-down version of Jesus and obeying him only partially, yet expecting to receive his full promise of guidance, protection, blessing, and even eternal life?

What adjustments must you make in your life in order to show full acknowledgment of Jesus as *the* way, *the* truth, and *the* life?

Jesus said, "When you have lifted up the Son of Man, then you will know that I am the one I claim to be" (John 8:28). Are you lifting up Jesus on a daily basis? If not, you may be struggling to accept Jesus' claims in John 14:6. Pause now to lift up Jesus in the silence of this moment. Journal your prayer below as you experience him as the only way, the only truth, and the only route to abundant life.

Wrapping It Up

Bringing Hope and Assurance Close to Home

Select the appropriate Teach It guide for your session (full Teach It guides are on the CD-ROM accompanying this book). Then read through the guide so you're familiar with the flow of the session and confident with each exercise. Be sure to allow time for printing or photocopying student pages and pulling together any materials needed (see the Materials step in the Teach It guide).

Before you close your book, read John 14:1-14 again. Ingest these words as if Jesus himself were speaking them to you... because he is. Listen for hope and assurance. Then pray for your group—that they will begin to experience the hope that comes when we believe in Jesus as the way, the truth, and the life.

WEB SUPPORT:
Remember to check out Web support for *See, Believe, Live* at www.inword.org. You'll find updated media suggestions (music, video clips), along with additional prep helps and even more application ideas. When at www.inword.org, look for the Digging Deeper series icon. You'll find password information in the Instructions at the front of this book.

John 14:1-31

1 "Do not let your hearts be troubled. Trust in God; trust also in me.

2 In my Father's house are many rooms; if it were not so, I would have told you. I am going there to prepare a place for you.

3 And if I go and prepare a place for you, I will come back and take you to be with me that you also may be where I am.

4 You know the way to the place where I am going."

5 Thomas said to him, "Lord, we don't know where you are going, so how can we know the way?"

6 Jesus answered, "I am the way and the truth and the life. No one comes to the Father except through me.

7 If you really knew me, you would know my Father as well. From now on, you do know him and have seen him."

8 Philip said, "Lord, show us the Father and that will be enough for us."

9 Jesus answered: "Don't you know me, Philip, even after I have been among you such a long time? Anyone who has seen me has seen the Father. How can you say, 'Show us the Father'?

10 Don't you believe that I am in the Father, and that the Father is in me? The words I say to you are not just my own. Rather, it is the Father, living in me, who is doing his work.

11 Believe me when I say that I am in the Father and the Father is in me; or at least believe on the evidence of the miracles themselves.

12 I tell you the truth, anyone who has faith in me will do what I have been doing. He will do even greater things than these, because I am going to the Father.

13 And I will do whatever you ask in my name, so that the Son may bring glory to the Father.

14 You may ask me for anything in my name, and I will do it.

15 If you love me, you will obey what I command.

16 And I will ask the Father, and he will give you another Counselor to be with you forever—

17 the Spirit of truth. The world cannot accept him, because it neither sees him nor knows him. But

you know him, for he lives with you and will be in you.

18 I will not leave you as orphans; I will come to you.

19 Before long, the world will not see me anymore, but you will see me. Because I live, you also will live.

20 On that day you will realize that I am in my Father, and you are in me, and I am in you.

21 Whoever has my commands and obeys them, he is the one who loves me. He who loves me will be loved by my Father, and I too will love him and show myself to him."

22 Then Judas (not Judas Iscariot) said, "But, Lord, why do you intend to show yourself to us and not to the world?"

23 Jesus replied, "If anyone loves me, he will obey my teaching. My Father will love him, and we will come to him and make our home with him.

24 He who does not love me will not obey my teaching. These words you hear are not my own; they belong to the Father who sent me.

25 All this I have spoken while still with you.

26 But the Counselor, the Holy Spirit, whom the Father will send in my name, will teach you all things and will remind you of everything I have said to you.

27 Peace I leave with you; my peace I give you. I do not give to you as the world gives. Do not let your hearts be troubled and do not be afraid.

28 You heard me say, 'I am going away and I am coming back to you.' If you loved me, you would be glad that I am going to the Father, for the Father is greater than I.

29 I have told you now before it happens, so that when it does happen you will believe.

30 I will not speak with you much longer, for the prince of this world is coming. He has no hold on me,

31 but the world must learn that I love the Father and that I do exactly what my Father has commanded me. Come now; let us leave."

1. Materials

For this session each student will need—
- the Session 10 Scripture sheet
- the student journal page for Session 10
- his or her own Bible, a pen, and a notebook

You'll also need—
- a whiteboard and markers
- a pack of colored pencils (at least one color per student)
- optional: projection presentation featuring famous farewell quotations

2. Session Intro

GOALS OF SESSION 10

As students experience this session, they will—
- discover why Jesus spent a lot of time toward the end of his life (spanning nearly five chapters in John's Gospel) in an intimate, intense conversation with his disciples.
- explore Jesus' exclusive claims about who he is.
- explore some lofty promises Jesus made.
- be challenged to meet the conditions required to enjoy these promises.

PRAYER

OPEN: *FAMOUS FAREWELLS*
Introduce the idea of Jesus' farewell words with these familiar farewells.

3. Digging In: *Words to Live By*

Group Dig: Explore John 14:1-14 to discover some of Jesus' biggest and best promises.

4. Cross-Checking: *Did He Say "Greater"?*

Personal Retreat: Use this personal retreat for students to better understand and apply these incredible promises.

5. Digging Deeper *Bold Claims, Bold Actions*

Personal Retreat: Experience Jesus as the way, the truth, and the life.

6. Taking It Inward: *Taking Jesus at His Word*

Group Interaction: Help students decide whether or not they *want* Jesus' promises.

7. Wrapping It Up: *Bringing Hope and Assurance Close to Home*

Challenge students to apply Jesus' incredible promises to immediate problems they're facing.

1. Materials

For this session each student will need—
- the Session 10 Scripture sheet
- the student journal page for Session 10
- his or her own Bible, a pen, and a notebook

You'll also need—
- a whiteboard and markers
- a pack of colored pencils (at least one color per student)
- optional: projection presentation featuring famous farewell quotations

2. Session Intro

GOALS OF SESSION 10
As students experience this session, they will—
- discover why Jesus spent a lot of time toward the end of his life (spanning nearly five chapters in John's Gospel) in an intimate, intense conversation with his disciples.
- explore Jesus' exclusive claims about who he is.
- explore some lofty promises Jesus made.
- be challenged to meet the conditions required to enjoy these promises.

PRAYER

OPEN: *FAMOUS FAREWELLS*
Introduce the idea of Jesus' farewell words with these familiar farewells.

3. Digging In: *Words to Live By*

Group Dig: Explore John 14:1-14 to discover some of Jesus' biggest and best promises.

4. Cross-Checking: *Did He Say "Greater"?*

Personal Retreat: Use this personal retreat for students to better understand and apply these incredible promises.

5. Digging Deeper: *Bold Claims, Bold Actions*

Personal Retreat: Experience Jesus as the way, the truth, and the life.

6. Taking It Inward: *Taking Jesus at His Word*

Group Interaction: Help students decide whether or not they *want* Jesus' promises.

7. Wrapping It Up: *Bringing Hope and Assurance Close to Home*

Challenge students to apply Jesus' incredible promises to immediate problems they're facing.

1. Materials

For this session each student will need—
- the Session 10 Scripture sheet
- the student journal page for Session 10
- his or her own Bible, a pen, and a notebook

You'll also need—
- a whiteboard and markers
- a pack of colored pencils (at least one color per student)
- optional: projection presentation featuring famous farewell quotations

2. Session Intro

GOALS OF SESSION 10
As students experience this session, they will—
- discover why Jesus spent a lot of time toward the end of his life (spanning nearly five chapters in John's Gospel) in an intimate, intense conversation with his disciples.
- explore Jesus' exclusive claims about who he is.
- explore some lofty promises Jesus made.
- be challenged to meet the conditions required to enjoy these promises.

PRAYER

OPEN: *FAMOUS FAREWELLS*
Introduce the idea of Jesus' farewell words with these familiar farewells.

3. Digging In: *Words to Live By*

Group Dig: Explore John 14:1-14 to discover some of Jesus' biggest and best promises.

4. Cross-Checking: *Did He Say "Greater"?*

Personal Retreat: Use this personal retreat for students to better understand and apply these incredible promises.

5. Digging Deeper: *Bold Claims, Bold Actions*

Personal Retreat: Experience Jesus as the way, the truth, and the life.

6. Taking It Inward: *Taking Jesus at His Word*

Group Interaction: Help students decide whether or not they *want* Jesus' promises.

7. Wrapping It Up: *Bringing Hope and Assurance Close to Home*

Challenge students to apply Jesus' incredible promises to immediate problems they're facing.

1. Materials

For this session each student will need—
- the Session 10 Scripture sheet
- the student journal page for Session 10
- his or her own Bible, a pen, and a notebook

You'll also need—
- a whiteboard and markers
- a pack of colored pencils (at least two colors per student)
- optional: projection presentation featuring famous farewell quotations

2. Session Intro

GOALS OF SESSION 10

As students experience this session, they will—
- discover why Jesus spent a lot of time toward the end of his life (spanning nearly five chapters in John's Gospel) in an intimate, intense conversation with his disciples.
- explore Jesus' exclusive claims about who he is.
- explore some lofty promises Jesus made.
- be challenged to meet the conditions required to enjoy these promises.

PRAYER

OPEN: *FAMOUS FAREWELLS*

Introduce the idea of Jesus' farewell words with these familiar farewells.

3. Digging In: *Words to Live By*

Group Dig: Dig out the different reasons Jesus is having this talk with his disciples.
Group Dig: Explore John 14:1-14 to discover some of Jesus' biggest and best promises.

4. Cross-Checking: *Did He Say "Greater"?*

Personal Retreat: Use this personal retreat for students to better understand and apply these incredible promises.

5. Digging Deeper: *Bold Claims, Bold Actions*

Personal Retreat: Experience Jesus as the way, the truth, and the life.

6. Taking It Inward: *Taking Jesus at His Word*

Group Interaction: Help students decide whether or not they *want* Jesus' promises.

7. Wrapping It Up: *Bringing Hope and Assurance Close to Home*

Challenge students to apply Jesus' incredible promises to immediate problems they're facing.

1. Materials

For this session each student will need—
- his or her own Bible
- optional: the student journal page for Session 10, including an "on your own" exercise (Using the student journal page is optional in the coffeehouse setting since table space will be limited.)

You'll also need—
- a pack of pencils with erasers
- optional: a few spare Bibles for students who've forgotten theirs
- optional: famous farewell quotations (printed or viewed on a laptop)

2. Session Intro

GOALS OF SESSION 10

As students experience this session, they will—
- discover why Jesus spent a lot of time toward the end of his life (spanning nearly five chapters in John's Gospel) in an intimate, intense conversation with his disciples.
- explore Jesus' exclusive claims about who he is.
- explore some lofty promises Jesus made.
- be challenged to meet the conditions required to enjoy these promises.

PRAYER

OPEN: *FAMOUS FAREWELLS*
Introduce the idea of Jesus' farewell words with these familiar farewells.

3. Digging In: *Words to Live By*

Group Dig: Explore John 14:1-14 to discover some of Jesus' biggest and best promises.

4. Cross-Checking: *Did He Say "Greater"?*

Group Dig: Help students better understand and apply these incredible promises.

5. Taking It Inward: *Taking Jesus at His Word*

Group Interaction: Help students decide whether or not they *want* Jesus' promises.

6. Wrapping It Up: *Bringing Hope and Assurance Close to Home*

Challenge students to apply Jesus' incredible promises to immediate problems they're facing.
On Your Own: Offer students the option of experiencing Jesus as the way, the truth, and the life with this "on your own" exercise.

1. Materials (Optional)
- Movie Trailer: The first 56 seconds of the trailer for *Twins,* featuring Arnold Schwarzenegger and Danny DeVito. Go to the Main Menu on the DVD, select Bonus Materials, and then select Theatrical Trailer. You may also be able to find the trailer online on a video-sharing Web site such as YouTube.
- A large mirror
- Quotations that relate to personal identity

2. Optional Opens
Movie Trailer: *Twins*
Visual Illustration: A mirror helps answer the question: Who am I—the real me, or the image I project?
Quotations: Notable quotations weigh in on what makes our personal and Christian identities.

3. Digging Deeper
Personal Story: Share about how your personal identity (or a friend's) has changed through life.
John 14:10-16
Promise: Jesus says we can do greater things than he, and that may not be too far-fetched.

4. Taking It Inward
Internalize Jesus' extravagant promises by picturing what they can look like in our lives.

5. Wrapping It Up
Challenge students to visualize themselves overcoming challenges and temptations because of their faith in Jesus.

SESSION 11

Setting the Heart

Have you ever wondered why God set things up the way he did? Why, for example, it took the shedding of blood to take away our sin?

Well for starters, *blood is everything*. With no blood in your body, everything that makes you *you* would cease to exist! Your personality, your emotions—everything about you is physically sustained by your blood. Blood is the bridge between the physical and the spiritual. It's what supports the physical body in order for the spiritual to have a place to dwell. The moment we cease to have enough healthy blood to sustain our physical bodies, our souls leave the physical world.

Doesn't it stand to reason that God—creator of both the physical *and* the spiritual—would use blood to bridge the gap between a fallen physical world and himself? In fact, God said, "For the life of the flesh is in the blood, and I have given it to you upon the altar to make atonement for your souls; for it is the blood that makes atonement for the soul" (Leviticus 17:11, NKJV). In order for sinful people to have a relationship with a holy God, blood must be shed for the cleansing of our sins. In Old Testament times, a lamb without defect was used to accomplish this cleansing. It was the blood of a lamb that allowed the death angel to "pass over" the homes of Israel just before they were delivered from slavery in Egypt (Exodus 12)—a vivid picture of God's "passing over" our transgressions by the blood of Jesus, when he delivers us from slavery to sin.

More than any other Gospel writer, John portrays Jesus as the Lamb of God. Depicting the events of Jesus' crucifixion, John intentionally reminds us of the season at hand—Passover, the annual celebration of Israel's protection from certain death by the blood of a spotless lamb.

Centuries before, Isaiah foretold Jesus' death as the sacrificial Lamb who takes away the sins of the world. Spend a moment preparing to witness Jesus' sacrifice by reading Isaiah's words.

> He was oppressed and afflicted, yet he did not open his mouth; he was led like a lamb to the slaughter, and as a sheep before her shearers is silent, so he did not open his mouth. By oppression and judgment he was taken away. And who can speak of his descendants? For he was cut off from the land of the living; for the transgression of my people he was stricken. He was assigned a grave with the wicked, and with the rich in his death, though he had done no violence, nor was any deceit in his mouth. (Isaiah 53:7-9)

Pre-Dig

First Blood

To experience maximum impact from the events of Jesus' trial and crucifixion, we need to do some background work. Jesus' sacrifice was the ultimate act in God's plan to redeem a fallen world through the shedding of blood. To better understand what it meant for Jesus to be called the Lamb of God, read about the lamb at the first Passover in Exodus 12:1-27. If you're comfortable marking in your Bible, circle the word *lamb* (along with any synonyms) wherever it appears. Then note below everything you learn about the lamb and what its blood meant for Israel's families.

The Lamb

What did the blood of the lamb protect the households of Israel from?

What did the Lord do when he saw the blood on the doorposts of a home? (Use the words your Bible uses to describe this action in Exodus 12:13, 23, and 27.)

Digging In

Power-Play Ploy

Now fast-forward to John 18. By this time, the Jewish leaders could see only one solution to the Jesus problem: *execute him*. But the Jews had no authority to execute someone condemned to die by their own law. To carry out capital punishment, they needed the rubber stamp of a Roman official—which is why the proceedings moved to Pilate's palace, where the Jewish leaders revealed to what extent they were willing to go to rid themselves of Jesus.

Though you won't cover every stage of Jesus' trial with your students, you'll want to be familiar with the details. Read John 18:28–19:16 from your Scripture sheet. As you read, record in the left column below the Jews' actions and reactions toward Pilate. In the right column, record Pilate's corresponding actions and reactions, aligning these with the facts in the left column. When you've finished, you should have a concise outline of the power play between Pilate and the Jewish leaders.

The Jews	Pilate

What ploys did the Jewish leaders use to coerce Pilate into having Jesus killed?

In what ways did Pilate try to appease the Jewish leaders, while trying to avoid having Jesus put to death?

In order to execute Jesus, what were the Jews apparently willing to give up?

Let's say you're a political reporter who's in Jerusalem to cover this tumultuous Passover. How would you assess the interaction between the Jewish leaders and Pilate? What did the Jews give up in order to gain what they wanted? What was Pilate willing to give up?

Digging Deeper

"Corrupt and Conniving" Meets "Undefiled and Spotless"

A corrupt, conniving faction coerces a weak-willed official to execute Jesus, whom Scripture describes as an undefiled, spotless Lamb. *Let the sacrifice begin.*

Now read John 19:1-37 from your Scripture sheet.

> As you read, circle every phrase that describes an action done to Jesus' physical body, such as an act that may have drawn blood.

After you've finished, list below precisely what the people did to Jesus.

What They Did to Jesus

Taking It Inward

Broken and Spilled

You've just witnessed the highest injustice...the supreme act of love...the greatest sacrifice of all time. Maybe it's been a while since you've pondered the sacrifice Jesus made for you. Take a moment to reflect on what was done to Jesus—and remember that it was all done with you in mind. While the experience is fresh in your mind, pause to worship the Lamb of God, whose blood was poured out for you.

Now refresh your memory of Exodus 12 and the account of the first Passover. What parallels do you see between that sacrifice and Jesus' death on the cross?

The passages below remind us of the connection between the Passover sacrifice and the Lamb of God. As you read these, list everything you learn about Jesus as the sacrificial Lamb.

John 1:29

1 Peter 1:18-21

Revelation 5:9-13

The application of this scene is very personal—no challenge to "change the world" or even to "change your community." Instead, we want you to make an internal application as you consider your relationship with Jesus, the sacrificial Lamb. In 1 Peter 1, Peter goes on to instruct us about how Jesus' sacrifice should impact our personal lives. Read 1 Peter 1:22–2:3 from your Bible. As you read, make two lists: 1) benefits you've received as a result of Jesus' sacrifice, and 2) what your behavior should look like because of Jesus' sacrifice.

Benefits	Behavior

What connections do you see between the behavior and benefits you listed?

How has Jesus' sacrifice changed the way you love people or deal with deceit in your life?

Look again at 1 Peter 2:2-3. As a believer, you've tasted the goodness of the Lord. Are you letting this "taste" lead to the craving Peter described?

Wrapping It Up

Name Drop

Select the appropriate Teach It guide for your session (full Teach It guides are on the CD-ROM accompanying this book). Then read the guide so you're familiar with the flow of the session and confident with each exercise. Be sure to allow time for printing or photocopying student pages and pulling together any materials needed (see the Materials step in the Teach It guide).

It's too bad that in many churches, "the blood of Jesus" has become a cliché. Yet his blood is our lifeline. As we said at the start, the blood is *everything*. Just imagine Jesus' blood pouring down his body—from the nails, the crown, the spear, the slaps, and the floggings. At the base of the cross, a pool of blood is forming—and in that pool is a drop of blood with your name on it, as well as drops with the names of your students. Pray for each student now, that they'll gain a fresh appreciation for the sacrifice of God's undefiled Lamb.

WEB SUPPORT:
Remember to check out Web support for *See, Believe, Live* at www.inword.org. You'll find updated media suggestions (music, video clips), along with additional prep helps and even more application ideas. When at www.inword.org, look for the Digging Deeper series icon. You'll find password information in the Instructions at the front of this book.

John 18:28-40

28 Then the Jews led Jesus from Caiaphas to the palace of the Roman governor. By now it was early morning, and to avoid ceremonial uncleanness the Jews did not enter the palace; they wanted to be able to eat the Passover.

29 So Pilate came out to them and asked, "What charges are you bringing against this man?"

30 "If he were not a criminal," they replied, "we would not have handed him over to you."

31 Pilate said, "Take him yourselves and judge him by your own law." "But we have no right to execute anyone," the Jews objected.

32 This happened so that the words Jesus had spoken indicating the kind of death he was going to die would be fulfilled.

33 Pilate then went back inside the palace, summoned Jesus and asked him, "Are you the king of the Jews?"

34 "Is that your own idea," Jesus asked, "or did others talk to you about me?"

35 "Am I a Jew?" Pilate replied. "It was your people and your chief priests who handed you over to me. What is it you have done?"

36 Jesus said, "My kingdom is not of this world. If it were, my servants would fight to prevent my arrest by the Jews. But now my kingdom is from another place."

37 "You are a king, then!" said Pilate. Jesus answered, "You are right in saying I am a king. In fact, for this reason I was born, and for this I came into the world, to testify to the truth. Everyone on the side of truth listens to me."

38 "What is truth?" Pilate asked. With this he went out again to the Jews and said, "I find no basis for a charge against him.

39 But it is your custom for me to release to you one prisoner at the time of the Passover. Do you want me to release 'the king of the Jews'?"

40 They shouted back, "No, not him! Give us Barabbas!" Now Barabbas had taken part in a rebellion.

John 19:1-37

1   Then Pilate took Jesus and had him flogged.

2   The soldiers twisted together a crown of thorns and put it on his head. They clothed him in a purple robe

3   and went up to him again and again, saying, "Hail, king of the Jews!" And they struck him in the face.

4   Once more Pilate came out and said to the Jews, "Look, I am bringing him out to you to let you know that I find no basis for a charge against him."

5   When Jesus came out wearing the crown of thorns and the purple robe, Pilate said to them, "Here is the man!"

6   As soon as the chief priests and their officials saw him, they shouted, "Crucify! Crucify!" But Pilate answered, "You take him and crucify him. As for me, I find no basis for a charge against him."

7   The Jews insisted, "We have a law, and according to that law he must die, because he claimed to be the Son of God."

8   When Pilate heard this, he was even more afraid,

9   and he went back inside the palace. "Where do you come from?" he asked Jesus, but Jesus gave him no answer.

10 "Do you refuse to speak to me?" Pilate said. "Don't you realize I have power either to free you or to crucify you?"

11 Jesus answered, "You would have no power over me if it were not given to you from above. Therefore the one who handed me over to you is guilty of a greater sin."

12 From then on, Pilate tried to set Jesus free, but the Jews kept shouting, "If you let this man go, you are no friend of Caesar. Anyone who claims to be a king opposes Caesar."

13 When Pilate heard this, he brought Jesus out and sat down on the judge's seat at a place known as the Stone Pavement (which in Aramaic is Gabbatha).

14 It was the day of Preparation of Passover Week, about the sixth hour. "Here is your king," Pilate said to the Jews.

15 But they shouted, "Take him away! Take him away! Crucify him!" "Shall I crucify your king?" Pilate

asked. "We have no king but Caesar," the chief priests answered.

16 Finally Pilate handed him over to them to be crucified. So the soldiers took charge of Jesus.

17 Carrying his own cross, he went out to the place of the Skull (which in Aramaic is called Golgotha).

18 Here they crucified him, and with him two others—one on each side and Jesus in the middle.

19 Pilate had a notice prepared and fastened to the cross. It read: JESUS OF NAZARETH, THE KING OF THE JEWS.

20 Many of the Jews read this sign, for the place where Jesus was crucified was near the city, and the sign was written in Aramaic, Latin and Greek.

21 The chief priests of the Jews protested to Pilate, "Do not write 'The King of the Jews,' but that this man claimed to be king of the Jews."

22 Pilate answered, "What I have written, I have written."

23 When the soldiers crucified Jesus, they took his clothes, dividing them into four shares, one for each of them, with the undergarment remaining. This garment was seamless, woven in one piece from top to bottom.

24 "Let's not tear it," they said to one another. "Let's decide by lot who will get it." This happened that the scripture might be fulfilled which said, "They divided my garments among them and cast lots for my clothing." So this is what the soldiers did.

25 Near the cross of Jesus stood his mother, his mother's sister, Mary the wife of Clopas, and Mary Magdalene.

26 When Jesus saw his mother there, and the disciple whom he loved standing nearby, he said to his mother, "Dear woman, here is your son,"

27 and to the disciple, "Here is your mother." From that time on, this disciple took her into his home.

28 Later, knowing that all was now completed, and so that the Scripture would be fulfilled, Jesus said, "I am thirsty."

29 A jar of wine vinegar was there, so they soaked a sponge in it, put the sponge on a stalk of the hyssop plant, and lifted it to Jesus' lips.

30 When he had received the drink, Jesus said, "It is finished." With that, he bowed his head and gave up his spirit.

31 Now it was the day of Preparation, and the next day was to be a special Sabbath. Because the Jews

did not want the bodies left on the crosses during the Sabbath, they asked Pilate to have the legs broken and the bodies taken down.

32 The soldiers therefore came and broke the legs of the first man who had been crucified with Jesus, and then those of the other.

33 But when they came to Jesus and found that he was already dead, they did not break his legs.

34 Instead, one of the soldiers pierced Jesus' side with a spear, bringing a sudden flow of blood and water.

35 The man who saw it has given testimony, and his testimony is true. He knows that he tells the truth, and he testifies so that you also may believe.

36 These things happened so that the scripture would be fulfilled: "Not one of his bones will be broken,"

37 and, as another scripture says, "They will look on the one they have pierced."

1. Materials

For this session each student will need—
- the Session 11 Scripture sheet
- the student journal page for Session 11
- his or her own Bible, a pen, and a notebook

You'll also need—
- a whiteboard and markers
- a pack of colored pencils (at least one color per student)
- several shopping bags (one per group of students) containing bridge-building materials: a newspaper (a Sunday edition is best), 10 pipe cleaners, 10 straws, 10 paper clips, and 10 tongue depressors or Popsicle sticks
- scissors (one pair per group of students)
- one brick or hymnal per group
- optional: prizes for the team with the best bridge
- optional: grape juice, bread, small cups, and a basket or plate for communion (See the Optional Close in Wrapping It Up.)

2. Session Intro

GOALS OF SESSION 11

As students experience this session, they will—
- examine the details of Jesus' trial and crucifixion.
- gain understanding of Jesus as the sacrificial Lamb of God.
- be challenged to make Jesus' sacrifice a motivation for living life in a different way.

PRAYER

OPEN: *BRIDGE MAKING*
Use this bridge-building contest to introduce the bridges God has used in the past.

3. Pre-Dig: *First Blood*

Group Dig: Explore Exodus 12:1-15 to see why blood is part of the deal.

4. Digging In: *"Corrupt and Conniving" Meets "Undefiled and Spotless"*

Group Dig: Explore John 19:1-37 to look in on an unjust trial and create a step-by-step picture of the physical pain inflicted on Jesus.

5. Taking It Inward: *Broken and Spilled*

Personal Retreat: These verses will serve as the big "put together" in understanding why Jesus did what he did.

6. Wrapping It Up: *Name Drop*

Group Interaction: This discussion will help students take Jesus' blood personally.
Optional Close: Experience the Lord's Supper together.

1. Materials

For this session each student will need—
- the Session 11 Scripture sheet
- the student journal page for Session 11
- his or her own Bible, a pen, and a notebook

You'll also need—
- a whiteboard and markers
- a pack of colored pencils (at least one color per student)
- images of famous or local bridges (printed or projected)
- optional: grape juice, bread, small cups, and a basket or plate for communion (See the Optional Close in Wrapping It Up.)

2. Session Intro

GOALS OF SESSION 11
As students experience this session, they will—
- examine the details of Jesus' trial and crucifixion.
- gain understanding of Jesus as the sacrificial Lamb of God.
- be challenged to make Jesus' sacrifice a motivation for living life in a different way.

PRAYER

OPEN: *NAME THAT BRIDGE*
Group Game: Print or project images of famous or local bridges for students to guess. Use this contest to introduce the bridges God has used in the past.

3. Pre-Dig: *First Blood*

Group Dig: Explore Exodus 12:1-15 to see why blood is part of the deal.

4. Digging In: *"Corrupt and Conniving" Meets "Undefiled and Spotless"*

Explore John 19:1-37 to look in on an unjust trial and create a step-by-step picture of the physical pain inflicted on Jesus.

5. Taking It Inward: *Broken and Spilled*

Personal Retreat: These verses will serve as the big "put together" in understanding why Jesus did what he did.

6. Wrapping It Up: *Name Drop*

Group Interaction: This discussion will help students take Jesus' blood personally.
Optional Close: Experience the Lord's Supper together.

JOHN 18-19
PILATE'S PLOT

1. Materials

For this session each student will need—
- the Session 11 Scripture sheet
- the student journal page for Session 11
- his or her own Bible, a pen, and a notebook

You'll also need—
- a whiteboard and markers
- a pack of colored pencils (at least two colors per student)
- images of famous or local bridges (printed or projected)
- optional: grape juice, bread, small cups, and a basket or plate for communion (See the Optional Close in Wrapping It Up.)

2. Session Intro

GOALS OF SESSION 11

As students experience this session, they will—
- examine the details of Jesus' trial and crucifixion.
- gain understanding of Jesus as the sacrificial Lamb of God.
- be challenged to make Jesus' sacrifice a motivation for living life in a different way.

PRAYER

OPEN: *NAME THAT BRIDGE*

Group Game: Print or project images of famous or local bridges for students to guess. Use this contest to introduce the bridges God has used in the past.

3. Pre-Dig: *First Blood*

Group Dig: Explore Exodus 12:1-15 to see why blood is part of the deal.

4. Digging In: *Power-Play Ploy*

Group Dig: Explore John 18:28–19:16 to understand the power play between Pilate and the Jewish leaders.

5. Digging Deeper: *"Corrupt and Conniving" Meets "Undefiled and Spotless"*

Explore John 19:1-37 to look in on an unjust trial and create a step-by-step picture of the physical pain inflicted on Jesus.

6. Taking It Inward: *Broken and Spilled*

Personal Retreat: These verses will serve as the big "put together" in understanding why Jesus did what he did.

7. Wrapping It Up: *Name Drop*

Group Interaction: This discussion will help students take Jesus' blood personally.
Optional Close: Experience the Lord's Supper together.

1. Materials

For this session each student will need—
- the Session 11 Scripture sheet
- the student journal page for Session 11
- his or her own Bible, a pen, and a notebook

You'll also need—
- a whiteboard and markers
- a pack of colored pencils (at least two colors per student)
- images of famous or local bridges (printed or projected)
- optional: grape juice, bread, small cups, and a basket or plate for communion (See the Optional Close in Wrapping It Up.)

2. Session Intro

GOALS OF SESSION 11

As students experience this session, they will—
- examine the details of Jesus' trial and crucifixion.
- gain understanding of Jesus as the sacrificial Lamb of God.
- be challenged to make Jesus' sacrifice a motivation for living life in a different way.

PRAYER

OPEN: *NAME THAT BRIDGE*

Group Game: Print or project images of famous or local bridges for students to guess. Use this contest to introduce the bridges God has used in the past.

3. Pre-Dig: *First Blood*

Group Dig: Explore Exodus 12:1-15 to see why blood is part of the deal.

4. Digging In: *Power Play Ploy*

Group Dig: Explore John 18:28–19:16 to understand the power play between Pilate and the Jewish leaders.

5. Digging Deeper: *"Corrupt and Conniving" Meets "Undefiled and Spotless"*

Explore John 19:1-37 to look in on an unjust trial and create a step-by-step picture of the physical pain inflicted on Jesus.

6. Taking It Inward: *Broken and Spilled*

Personal Retreat: These verses will serve as the big "put together" in understanding why Jesus did what he did.

7. Wrapping It Up: *Name Drop*

Group Interaction: This discussion will help students take Jesus' blood personally.
Optional Close: Experience the Lord's Supper together.

JOHN 18-19
PILATE'S PLOT

1. Materials

For this session each student will need—
- his or her own Bible
- optional: the student journal page for Session 11, including an "on your own" exercise (Using the student journal page is optional in the coffeehouse setting since table space will be limited.)

You'll also need—
- images of famous or local bridges (printed or viewed on a laptop)
- a pack of pencils with erasers
- optional: a few spare Bibles for students who've forgotten theirs

2. Session Intro

GOALS OF SESSION 11
As students experience this session, they will—
- examine the details of Jesus' trial and crucifixion.
- gain understanding of Jesus as the sacrificial Lamb of God.
- be challenged to make Jesus' sacrifice a motivation for living life in a different way.

PRAYER

OPEN: *NAME THAT BRIDGE*
Group Game: Print or view on a laptop images of famous or local bridges for students to guess. Use this contest to introduce the bridges God has used in the past.

3. Pre-Dig: *First Blood*

Group Dig: Explore Exodus 12:1-12 to see why blood is part of the deal.

4. Digging In: *Power-Play Ploy*

Group Dig: Explore John 18:28–19:16 to understand the power play between Pilate and the Jewish leaders.

5. Digging Deeper: *"Corrupt and Conniving" Meets "Undefiled and Spotless"*

Explore John 19:1-37 to look in on an unjust trial and create a step-by-step picture of the physical pain inflicted on Jesus.

6. Taking It Inward: *Broken and Spilled*

Personal Retreat: These verses will serve as the big "put together" in understanding why Jesus did what he did.

7. Wrapping It Up: *Name Drop*

Group Interaction: This discussion will help students take Jesus' blood personally.
Optional: Schedule a time to experience the Lord's Supper together.

1. Materials (Optional)

- Roll of red tickets: available at any office-supply store
- A pen or pencil for each student
- Video Clip: *The Passion of the Christ*. Here are some suggested counter cues:
    Chapter 16, 0:52:05, at the whipping post
    Chapter 26, 1:31:25, the walk to Golgotha
    Chapter 28, 1:40:57, hoisting of the cross
    You can also find clips on a video-sharing Web site.

2. Optional Opens

Visual Illustration: Pass out red tickets (and pens or pencils) to represent redemption.
Story: Share a story about a personal sacrifice.

3. Digging In

Jesus showed us what real love is.

4. Taking It Inward

Object Lesson: Use the red ticket to depict a drop of blood with your name on it.
Video Clip: trial and scourging scenes form *The Passion of the Christ*

5. Wrapping It Up

Challenge students that we have a choice: to accept the kingdom of sacrificial love or the kingdom of this world.

Setting the Heart

It takes some faith to believe in the Resurrection. But isn't it just like God to put all the eggs in the faith basket? Hebrews 11:6 says that without faith, it's impossible to please God. It stands to reason then that God would want us to take that plunge of faith and accept as reality what can only be described as miraculous. As you prepare your heart to explore the primo event of the Christian faith, take a moment to ask yourself the question Jesus asked Martha, just before he raised Lazarus from the dead.

> Jesus said to her, "I am the resurrection and the life. He who believes in me will live, even though he dies; and whoever lives and believes in me will never die. Do you believe this?" (John 11:25-26)

Pre-Dig

Crucifixion Observation

Read John 19:25-27 from either your Bible or your Session 11 Scripture sheet. Record below the people who witnessed Jesus' crucifixion.[6]

Now imagine the last image these people had of Jesus after he was crucified. You may want to list the physical damage that would have been visible on Jesus' body.

Digging In

Resurrection Revelation

It's safe to conclude that Jesus' followers were utterly convinced their master and friend was dead. As Friday faded into Saturday, their hopes that Jesus would conquer death surely faded.

---

6 Most scholars agree that the disciple "whom he loved" was John, the author of this Gospel.

Using your Scripture sheet, read John 20:1-18.

> As you read, watch for the words *saw* and *looked*, as well as any forms of these words. Mark these with a pair of eyes [eyes icon] or glasses [glasses icon]. Be sure to observe *who* was doing the seeing and *what* he or she saw.

Looking back at what you've marked, record in the chart what each person saw and how he or she responded. Be as detailed as possible.

Who saw?	What did he or she see?	How did he or she respond?

Taking It Inward

Resurrection Refutation

In the generations since Jesus' resurrection, many skeptics have offered theories to undermine the historical reality of this event. Listed below are three of these theories. Based on what you've observed in John 19–20, how would you refute them? Write your defense in the space provided.

1. Christ didn't actually die on the cross, but managed to escape and later appeared to the disciples.

2. The disciples stole Jesus' body (as the Jews claimed in Matthew 28:12-13) and concocted the post-Resurrection events recorded in Scripture.

3. Mary Magdalene and the disciples went to the wrong tomb.

What about you? What's your gut level belief about the Resurrection? Look again at the question Jesus asked Martha in John 11:26, just after he explained the incredible blessing of believing in his resurrection. *Do you believe?*

Picture the details Mary Magdalene and the disciples saw on that first day of the week, while it was still dark. Put your heart inside that scene—in those initial moments when it dawned on them that something wonderfully strange was happening. Listen to Jesus say your name, just as he said Mary's. Journal your impressions about the Resurrection.

There's no getting around the Resurrection. It's the centerpiece of the Christian faith. (Read 1 Corinthians 15 if you doubt this.) Therefore it's important to understand the weaknesses of various arguments that attempt to explain it away. The purpose of this session isn't to present a thorough defense of Jesus' physical resurrection. But if your students have questions, you may want to explore this further through the writings of Josh McDowell, William Lane Craig, and other apologists.

Digging Deeper

Resurrection Proclamation

In Romans 10:9 Paul writes, "...if you confess with your mouth, 'Jesus is Lord,' and believe in your heart that God raised him from the dead, you will be saved." Belief in Jesus' resurrection from the dead is imperative to the Christian faith; every New Testament book refers to the Resurrection explicitly or implicitly. Allow the Lord to speak to you about this miraculous event as you experience the passages below. In fact, slow down the pace for a few minutes. Grab a cup of coffee or a favorite beverage, and find a quiet place for some solitude. Listen to the Spirit as he teaches you about Christ's resurrection.

Acts 2:29-41
This passage records the first sermon preached after Jesus' resurrection. Write down the details Peter gave about Jesus' death and resurrection.

What did Jesus' resurrection declare him to be, once and for all? (See Acts 2:36.)

What effect did the message of the Resurrection have on Peter's listeners?

Acts 17:18-34
The Areopagus was a public square in ancient Athens where philosophers debated the ideas of the day. Paul was invited there to share about the Resurrection. Follow Paul's strategy as he lays out the tenets of the Christian faith using his listeners' language, including their own reasoning, philosophy, and poetry. Be sure to record the results of his speech.

Romans 6:1-14
Romans has been called the constitution of the Christian faith. As you read this foundational passage about Jesus' resurrection, use the Scriptures to answer the question below. (You should come up with quite a list!)

What did Christ's resurrection do for us?

1 Corinthians 15:12-44
As you read this passage, list the consequences we would be experiencing had Jesus not been raised from the dead.

Other Related Passages

If you have time, be sure to check out these incredible passages about the Resurrection. You won't deal with them in the group session, but they'll enrich your appreciation of this pivotal event.

Romans 1:1-6

Romans 8:11-13

Ephesians 1:18-21

Philippians 3:10-11

1 Peter 1:3-4

1 Peter 3:18-22

Taking It Inward

Resurrection Transformation

Belief equals action—or at least it should, going by the biblical definition of *belief*. What good is it to believe in something if it has no impact on your behavior? You can believe in exercise, but if you never get off the couch, what good is it? The bottom line is: If your belief doesn't translate into action, *can you really say you believe?* (See James 2:14-19 for the Bible's answer to this question.)

Apply this principle to your belief in Jesus' resurrection. Use the questions below to prayerfully confront the reality of the Resurrection in your life. Journal your thoughts beneath each question.

How am I taking advantage of the hope I've been given through the Resurrection?

How am I experiencing the blessings and promises of resurrection power, which God has exerted on and in me?

What difference is Jesus' resurrection making in my life? Am I walking in the newness of life that the Resurrection gives?

Wrapping It Up

Resurrection Action

Let's get hyper-practical. Take a moment to write down some specific actions you can take that would show the people around you—friends, family members, coworkers, students—that Jesus' resurrection is real. And need we say it? Don't just write them; *do them!*

Actions

Select the appropriate Teach It guide for your session (full Teach It guides are on the CD-ROM accompanying this book). Then read through the guide so you're familiar with the flow of the session and confident with each exercise. Be sure to allow time for printing or photocopying student pages and pulling together any materials needed (see the *Materials* step in the Teach It guide).

Take a few minutes to pray for your students by name, that they will see the reality of the Resurrection as never before.

WEB SUPPORT:
Remember to check out Web support for *See, Believe, Live* at www.inword.org. You'll find updated media suggestions (music, video clips), along with additional prep helps and even more application ideas. When at www.inword.org, look for the Digging Deeper series icon. You'll find password information in the Instructions at the front of this book.

John 20:1-31

1   Early on the first day of the week, while it was still dark, Mary Magdalene went to the tomb and saw that the stone had been removed from the entrance.

2   So she came running to Simon Peter and the other disciple, the one Jesus loved, and said, "They have taken the Lord out of the tomb, and we don't know where they have put him!"

3   So Peter and the other disciple started for the tomb.

4   Both were running, but the other disciple outran Peter and reached the tomb first.

5   He bent over and looked in at the strips of linen lying there but did not go in.

6   Then Simon Peter, who was behind him, arrived and went into the tomb. He saw the strips of linen lying there,

7   as well as the burial cloth that had been around Jesus' head. The cloth was folded up by itself, separate from the linen.

8   Finally the other disciple, who had reached the tomb first, also went inside. He saw and believed.

9   (They still did not understand from Scripture that Jesus had to rise from the dead.)

10 Then the disciples went back to their homes,

11 but Mary stood outside the tomb crying. As she wept, she bent over to look into the tomb

12 and saw two angels in white, seated where Jesus' body had been, one at the head and the other at the foot.

13 They asked her, "Woman, why are you crying?" "They have taken my Lord away," she said, "and I don't know where they have put him."

14 At this, she turned around and saw Jesus standing there, but she did not realize that it was Jesus.

15 "Woman," he said, "why are you crying? Who is it you are looking for?" Thinking he was the gardener, she said, "Sir, if you have carried him away, tell me where you have put him, and I will get him."

16 Jesus said to her, "Mary." She turned toward him and cried out in Aramaic, "Rabboni!" (which

means Teacher).

17 Jesus said, "Do not hold on to me, for I have not yet returned to the Father. Go instead to my brothers and tell them, 'I am returning to my Father and your Father, to my God and your God.'"

18 Mary Magdalene went to the disciples with the news: "I have seen the Lord!" And she told them that he had said these things to her.

19 On the evening of that first day of the week, when the disciples were together, with the doors locked for fear of the Jews, Jesus came and stood among them and said, "Peace be with you!"

20 After he said this, he showed them his hands and side. The disciples were overjoyed when they saw the Lord.

21 Again Jesus said, "Peace be with you! As the Father has sent me, I am sending you."

22 And with that he breathed on them and said, "Receive the Holy Spirit.

23 If you forgive anyone his sins, they are forgiven; if you do not forgive them, they are not forgiven."

24 Now Thomas (called Didymus), one of the Twelve, was not with the disciples when Jesus came.

25 So the other disciples told him, "We have seen the Lord!" But he said to them, "Unless I see the nail marks in his hands and put my finger where the nails were, and put my hand into his side, I will not believe it."

26 A week later his disciples were in the house again, and Thomas was with them. Though the doors were locked, Jesus came and stood among them and said, "Peace be with you!"

27 Then he said to Thomas, "Put your finger here; see my hands. Reach out your hand and put it into my side. Stop doubting and believe."

28 Thomas said to him, "My Lord and my God!"

29 Then Jesus told him, "Because you have seen me, you have believed; blessed are those who have not seen and yet have believed."

30 Jesus did many other miraculous signs in the presence of his disciples, which are not recorded in this book.

31 But these are written that you may believe that Jesus is the Christ, the Son of God, and that by believing you may have life in his name.

1. Materials

For this session each student will need—
- the Session 12 Scripture sheet
- the student journal page for Session 12
- his or her own Bible, a pen, and a notebook

You'll also need—
- a whiteboard and markers
- a pack of colored pencils (at least one color per student)
- printed or projected pictures of famous tombs found online through an image search
- camera or camera phone
- optional: a Bible, a picture or statue of praying hands, a "brain game" like a Rubik's Cube, and a microphone (See Wrapping It Up.)

2. Session Intro

GOALS OF SESSION 12
As students experience this session, they will—
- explore the details of Jesus' resurrection.
- be confronted with the reality and significance of the Resurrection.
- be challenged to personalize their belief in Jesus' resurrection.

PRAYER

OPEN: *DEFINING THE DEFINING EVENT*
Group Interaction: Show famous gravesites to introduce the subject of Jesus' tomb.

3. Digging In: *Resurrection Revelation*

Group Dig: Explore John 20:1-18 to see who saw what at the Resurrection.

4. Taking It Inward: *Resurrection Refutation*

Group Interaction: Discuss different conspiracy theories about Jesus' "supposed" resurrection.

5. Digging Deeper: *Resurrection Proclamation*

Personal Retreat: a look at Acts and Romans to see the *immediate* impact of the Resurrection

6. Taking It Inward: *Resurrection Transformation*

Personal Retreat: a look to see the *personal* impact of the Resurrection.

7. Wrapping It Up: *Resurrection Action*

Group Interaction: Encourage each other to let the Resurrection affect your lives.

Final Thoughts

Since this is your final session in John, spend a few minutes helping your students reflect on their study experience.

1. Materials

For this session each student will need—
- the Session 12 Scripture sheet
- the student journal page for Session 12
- his or her own Bible, a pen, and a notebook

You'll also need—
- slides or preprinted pictures of famous tombs found online through an image search
- a whiteboard and markers
- a pack of colored pencils (at least one color per student)
- "Resurrection Refutation" prompt cards
- objects to use as visual aids in the optional Wrapping It Up activity (a Bible, knee pads or a copy of *Pray* magazine, a "brain game" such as Sudoku, and something that connotes "rescue," such as a piece of rope, a roll of LifeSavers candy, or a life ring from a pool)

2. Session Intro

GOALS OF SESSION 12
As students experience this session, they will—
- explore the details of Jesus' resurrection.
- be confronted with the reality and significance of the Resurrection.
- be challenged to personalize their belief in Jesus' resurrection.

PRAYER

OPEN: *DEFINING THE DEFINING EVENT*
Group Interaction: Show famous gravesites to introduce the subject of Jesus' tomb.
Option: Do a contest with gravesite inscriptions (you can use the same list above).

3. Digging In: *Resurrection Revelation*

Group Dig: Explore John 20:1-18 to see who saw what at the Resurrection.

4. Taking It Inward: *Resurrection Refutation*

Group Interaction: Discuss different conspiracy theories about Jesus' "supposed" resurrection.

5. Digging Deeper: *Resurrection Proclamation*

Personal Retreat: a look at key passages to see the *immediate* impact of the Resurrection.

6. Taking It Inward: *Resurrection Transformation*

Personal Retreat: a look to see the *personal* impact of the Resurrection.

7. Wrapping It Up: *Resurrection Action*

Group Interaction: Encourage each other to let the Resurrection affect your lives.

Final Thoughts

Since this is your final session in John, spend a few minutes helping your students reflect on their study experience.

1. Materials

For this session each student will need—

- the Session 12 Scripture sheet
- the student journal page for Session 12
- his or her own Bible, a pen, and a notebook

You'll also need—

- a whiteboard and markers
- a pack of colored pencils (at least one color per student)

2. Session Intro

GOALS OF SESSION 12

As students experience this session, they will—

- explore the details of Jesus' resurrection.
- be confronted with the reality and significance of the Resurrection.
- be challenged to personalize their belief in Jesus' resurrection.

PRAYER

OPEN: *DEFINING THE DEFINING EVENT*
Group Interaction: Brainstorm Christianity's defining moments.

3. Digging In: *Resurrection Revelation*

Group Dig: Explore John 20:1-18 to see who saw what at the Resurrection.

4. Taking It Inward: *Resurrection Refutation*

Group Interaction: Discuss different conspiracy theories about Jesus' "supposed" resurrection.

5. Digging Deeper: *Resurrection Proclamation*

Personal Retreat: a look at key passages to see the *immediate* impact of the Resurrection.

6. Taking It Inward: *Resurrection Transformation*

Personal Retreat: a look to see the *personal* impact of the Resurrection.

7. Wrapping It Up: *Resurrection Action*

Group Interaction: Encourage each other to let the Resurrection affect your lives.

Final Thoughts

Since this is your final session in John, spend a few minutes helping your students reflect on their study experience.

1. Materials

For this session each student will need—
- the Session 12 Scripture sheet
- the student journal page for Session 12
- his or her own Bible, a pen, and a notebook

You'll also need—
- a whiteboard and markers
- a pack of colored pencils (at least two colors per student)
- optional: DVD of Discovery Channel's documentary, *The Lost Tomb of Jesus*
- optional: article about the lost tomb of Jesus, http://benwitherington.blogspot.com/2007/02/jesus-tomb-titanic-talpiot-tomb-theory.html

2. Session Intro

GOALS OF SESSION 12
As students experience this session, they will—
- explore the details of Jesus' resurrection.
- be confronted with the reality and significance of the Resurrection.
- be challenged to personalize their belief in Jesus' resurrection.

PRAYER

OPEN: *DEFINING THE DEFINING EVENT*
Group Interaction: Brainstorm Christianity's defining moments.

3. Digging In: *Resurrection Revelation*

Group Dig: Explore John 20:1-18 to see who saw what at the Resurrection.

4. Taking It Inward: *Resurrection Refutation*

Group Interaction: Discuss different conspiracy theories about Jesus' "supposed" resurrection.
Optional Group Interaction: Discuss the documentary *The Lost Tomb of Jesus*.

5. Digging Deeper: *Resurrection Proclamation*

Personal Retreat: a look at key passages to see the *immediate* impact of the Resurrection.

6. Taking It Inward: *Resurrection Transformation*

Personal Retreat: a look to see the *personal* impact of the Resurrection.

7. Wrapping It Up: *Resurrection Action*

Group Interaction: Encourage each other to let the Resurrection affect your lives.

Final Thoughts

Since this is your final session in John, spend a few minutes helping your students reflect on their study experience.

1. Materials

For this session each student will need—
- his or her own Bible
- optional: the student journal page for Session 12 (Using the student journal page is optional in the coffeehouse setting since table space will be limited.)

You'll also need—
- a pack of pencils with erasers
- optional: a few spare Bibles for students who've forgotten theirs

2. Session Intro

GOALS OF SESSION 12

As students experience this session, they will—
- explore the details of Jesus' resurrection.
- be confronted with the reality and significance of the Resurrection.
- be challenged to personalize their belief in Jesus' resurrection.

PRAYER

OPEN: *DEFINING THE DEFINING EVENT*
Group Interaction: Brainstorm Christianity's defining moments.

3. Digging In: *Resurrection Revelation*

Group Dig: Explore John 20:1-18 to see who saw what at the Resurrection.

4. Taking It Inward: *Resurrection Refutation*

Group Interaction: Discuss different conspiracy theories about Jesus' "supposed" resurrection.

5. Digging Deeper: *Resurrection Proclamation*

Group Dig: a look at key passages to see the *immediate* impact of the Resurrection.

6. Taking It Inward: *Resurrection Transformation*

Personal Retreat: a look to see the *personal* impact of the Resurrection.

7. Wrapping It Up: *Resurrection Action*

Group Interaction: Encourage each other to let the Resurrection affect your lives.

Final Thoughts

Since this is your final session in John, spend a few minutes helping your students reflect on their study experience.

1. Materials (Optional)

- Movie Trailer: *Awakenings*, based on Oliver Sacks' memoir of the same name. This film tells the true story of a doctor (Oliver Sacks, fictionalized as Malcolm Sayer, played by Robin Williams in the movie) who in 1969 discovered beneficial effects of a new drug, L-Dopa. Sacks used this drug with catatonic patients who survived the 1917–1928 epidemic of encephalitis lethargica, a disease that left patients in a statue-like condition, speechless and motionless. In the movie, Leonard Lowe (played by Robert De Niro) and other patients are awakened after decades in a catatonic state and must deal with a new life in a new time. The trailer is not on certain DVD versions but may be available online at video-sharing Web sites, such as http://youtube.com/watch?v=puJCjUsgq7o
- A pair of crutches or a wheelchair

2. Optional Opens

Movie Trailer: *Awakenings*
Visual Illustration: Start your talk on crutches or in a wheelchair to depict being bound to something. Consider doing your entire talk from the wheelchair, staying seated until you talk about what the power of the Resurrection has done for us.

3. Digging In

Personal Story: Share a story that involves experiencing freedom.
John 20:3-8
Romans 8:11
Resurrection power in us will change everything.

4. Taking It Inward

Philippians 4:8

5. Wrapping It Up

Challenge students to let the Resurrection power at work in them give them freedom from the things that hold them back.

The Middle School Survival Series books are filled with short and easy-to-read tips, along with funny stories from the authors (who, believe it or not, used to be middle school morons!), and quotes and questions from students like you. Focusing on issues you face at school, in your family, with friends, faith, and more, you'll learn a lot while you laugh out loud.

My Friends
ISBN 978-0-310-27881-8

My Changes
ISBN 978-0-310-27883-2

My Faith
ISBN 978-0-310-27382-0

My Future
ISBN 978-0-310-27884-9

My Family
ISBN 978-0-310-27430-8

Mark Oestreicher and Scott Rubin
RETAIL $9.99 ea.

My School
ISBN 978-0-310-27882-5

Kurt Johnston and Mark Oestreicher
RETAIL $9.99 ea.

invert

Visit www.invertbooks.com or your local bookstore.

The Wisdom On… series is designed to help you apply biblical wisdom to your everyday life. You'll find case studies, personal inventories, interactive activities, and helpful insights from the book of Proverbs, which will show you what wise living looks like.

Wisdom On...Friends, Dating, and Relationships
ISBN 978-0-310-27927-3
Wisdom On...Getting Along with Parents
ISBN 978-0-310-27929-7
Wisdom On...Growing in Christ
ISBN 978-0-310-27932-7
Wisdom On...Making Good Decisions
ISBN 978-0-310-27926-6
Wisdom On...Music, Movies, and Television
ISBN 978-0-310-27931-0
Wisdom On...Time & Money
ISBN 978-0-310-27928-0

Mark Matlock
RETAIL $9.99 ea.

invert

Students today are bombarded with opinions and research about Jesus that goes against everything you've been trying to teach them. They don't know if they can trust what the Bible says about Jesus because they don't know they can trust the Bible. They wonder if he really rose from the dead, or if he was even God. Let Lee Strobel's investigations into the real Jesus help your students see the truth about the Son of God.

The Case for the Real Jesus—Student Edition
A Journalist Investigates Current Challenges to Christianity
Lee Strobel with Jane Vogel
RETAIL $9.99
ISBN 978-0-310-28323-2

Visit www.invertbooks.com or your local bookstore.

Student Life Devotional Series

The Old Testament is full of characters. Spend 48 weeks looking more closely at those characters, and discover more about the character of the God who created us to be part of his story. With daily scripture and thoughts, questions to get you thinking, and plenty of space for you to journal your thoughts, you'll better understand how you fit into the story.

Character
Old Testament People, Encounters with God
Richard Parker
RETAIL $12.99
ISBN 978-0-310-27906-8

Jesus is one of the best-known people in history. But do you really know him? Spend 48 weeks looking at the life of Jesus and discover how he can impact your life. With daily scripture and thoughts, questions to get you thinking, and plenty of space for you to journal your thoughts, you'll get to know the real Jesus, and how you can become more like him.

Christ
The Life of Christ, The Basics of Life
Dr. Johnny Derouen
RETAIL $12.99
ISBN 978-0-310-27905-1

The Church started more than 2,000 years ago, but it still has relevance to us today. Spend 48 weeks looking more closely at the community of the Church. With daily scripture and thoughts, questions to get you thinking, and plenty of space for you to journal your thoughts, you'll find that the Church is more than a building—it's a family.

Community
The New Testament Church, The Essence of Fellowship
Adam Robinson
RETAIL $12.99
ISBN 978-0-310-27907-5

youth specialties

visit www.youthspecialties.com/store
or your local Christian bookstore